contents

Our primary purpose as Christians is to glorify God. So my question is: *Are you glorifying God in everything you do?* My prayer is that you would be a godly young woman. I want you to be a young woman who understands what is truly important in this life. I also want to see you seek the Lord, reject wrong and harmful behavior, point others toward Him with your actions and your words, and make a difference in this world for His kingdom. The woman portrayed in Proverbs 31 is a great example for us. I hope you learn as much as I did about being a godly woman during your own study of *Her*.

INTRODUCTION

That's *her*. Why can't I look like *her*? What makes *her* so special? I want to be like *her*.

You hear about *her* all the time. Who is she anyway? In this book, the *Her* we're referring to is the woman in Proverbs 31.

But it's also you.

We want you to see in yourself the seeds God has planted for you to become a young woman who knows Him, owns her faith in Him, and makes Him known. After all, He sees *Her* in you.

HOW TO USE THIS STUDY:

Each week you will study a different section of Proverbs 31. You will begin with an overall introduction to that week's theme. On the first day of each week, you'll study a part of Proverbs 31 in depth. Then, you'll discover more about the principle to be learned in that section of Scripture by looking at that topic elsewhere in the Bible throughout the rest of the week's study. There's a memory verse to learn each week, a lot of questions for you to think about, and plenty for you to journal about in this book. I hope that each day of this study you get a little closer to being *Her* . . . the godly young woman God created you to be!

Who can find
a capable wife?
She is far more precious
than jewels.

—Proverbs 31:10

week 1
the basics

INTRODUCTION TO WEEK 1

Proverbs 31 was written as a poem of instruction for young men. The writer was telling young men about the qualities they should look for in a wife. Many of you probably hope to be someone's wife one day. Don't you think it's important to know some qualities that all guys worth marrying are looking for in the woman they want to marry?

It's kind of like knowing the questions before you go in for a test. When you've studied and know the material, then taking the test—and doing well—is a whole lot easier than if you hadn't prepared. (But don't hear me say that taking a test or deciding whom to marry is easy!)

Even if you're not interested in getting married someday or already know God has called you to a life of singleness, Proverbs 31 isn't a chapter of Scripture you should skip. The verses describe the characteristics of a godly woman, and there are lessons for you within them. If you want to be a woman after God's own heart, the kind of woman He honors, Proverbs 31 is a good place to start.

Before you give up on trying to measure up to the Proverbs 31 woman, understand that the woman described in the proverb we'll study isn't real; she's an embodiment of every good quality in a woman. You should strive to be like her, but you don't have to try to do everything she managed to do.

THIS WEEK'S THEME

This week's study of Proverbs 31 will focus on **wisdom**. You'll discover what it is, why you need it, how to ask for it, and how to live wisely. The Proverbs are wisdom literature, as are the books of Job, Ecclesiastes, and Song of Songs. "Wisdom literature" is basically just a term used to describe a genre of writing used in Old Testament times to offer insight about life and how to live. It is usually characterized by sayings that teach about God, virtue, and life itself.

So what about you? Do you desire wisdom? Do you want to know that you're making the right decision? Look up James 1:5. What does it say?

> "Now if any of you lacks wisdom, he should ask God, who gives to all generously and without criticizing, and it will be given to him." —James 1:5

In James 1:5, we are told that "if we lack wisdom, we should ask God, who gives to all generously and without criticizing," and it will be given to us! So even if you've asked before, you may not be feeling very wise or capable of making wise decisions right now. That's OK! One of the ways we know how to make wise decisions is by studying the Bible. When we see how others handled situations and how God worked through them, it can be a little easier to know what to do in the situations we face.

That's why during this Bible study you're going to get into the Word. You're going to dig into Scripture. You'll have Scripture to read each day and questions to journal about. You're going to be asked to wrestle with the Word of God and what it means to be a Proverbs 31 kind of girl. Ultimately, you will walk away from this study with a better knowledge of the Bible and a better understanding of the incredible God we worship.

And because this study is also a journal, you'll have a written record of what you learned and what God did in your life to look back on when being a Proverbs 31 girl seems next to impossible.

FIRST THINGS FIRST

You've read the Bible before, right? Since it wasn't originally written in English, some of the things that make it beautiful were lost in translation. However, one of those literary devices is preserved in the passage we'll study. Proverbs 31 is a wisdom poem, and it's written as an acrostic in chiastic structure.

Now, you know what a poem is, and you likely know what an acrostic is. (For example, taking your name and coming up with a word that describes you, beginning with each letter in your name.) But this proverb, written in Hebrew, originally started each verse with a successive letter of the Hebrew alphabet. Even more impressive is the writer's ability to work that acrostic into a chiastic structure. A *chiasmus* (or something written in chiastic structure) is a literary device in which words, grammatical constructions, or ideas are given once and then repeated in reverse order. Sound complicated? It's really not. A simple example would be "I eat to live while she lives to eat." But in this passage, you'll find that the chiasmus looks like this:

- A: The value of a good wife (v. 10)
  - B: Wife benefits husband (vv. 11-12)
    - C: Wife works hard (vv. 13-19)
      - D: Wife reaches out to poor (v. 20)
        - E: No worry of weather (v. 21a)
          - F: Family clothed in quality goods (v. 21b)
            - G: Wife creates clothing and material out of fine fabric (v. 22)
              - H: Husband is publicly respected (v. 23)
            - G: Wife sells clothing and material made of fine fabric (v. 24)
          - F: Wife clothed in strength and honor (v. 25a)
        - E: No worry about the future (v. 25b)
      - D: Wife reaches out with wisdom (v. 26)
    - C: Wife works hard (v. 27)
  - B: Wife benefits the family, who praise her (v. 28-29)
- A: The value of a good wife (v. 31)

Ready to dive into week one? Let's get into the basics of wisdom.

day 1

Introducing the Proverbs 31 woman

Let's start off by reading the Proverb we'll be studying. **Read Proverbs 31, beginning with verse 10.**

- What stood out to you about the woman?

- What surprised you about her?

- What did you like about her?

- What didn't you like?

- Why do you think her husband married her?

Focus on verse 10 for a moment. In what ways would a woman be more precious than jewels to her husband?

GOING DEEPER:

Over the next several weeks we're going to learn a lot from this woman: being trustworthy, working hard with diligence and excellence, showing concern for others, being prepared, marrying wisely, controlling what comes out of our mouths, loving and respecting our families, and fearing the Lord. Each week we'll tackle a few verses from Proverbs 31 and many others throughout the Bible to see the truths God has for us. It is those truths that will help shape us into the women God wants us to be.

So think about it: What do you hope to get out of this Bible study? What characteristics do you want to embody at the end? If parts of your life are not pleasing to God, how do you want them to be different when you finish this Bible study? Journal about that in the space provided. Be specific. You may even want to write your thoughts as a prayer of commitment.

WEEKLY MEMORY VERSE:

"Now if any of you lacks wisdom, he should ask God, who gives to all generously and without criticizing, and it will be given to him. But let him ask in faith without doubting. For the doubter is like the surging sea, driven and tossed by the wind. That person should not expect to receive anything from the Lord. An indecisive man is unstable in all his ways."
—James 1:5-8

day 2

What's the point of studying Proverbs?

As we discussed before, Proverbs was written for young men. Think of it as a textbook for living. Since it was written with young men in mind, you'll find a lot of references to "young men," "my son," or "men." But don't think it doesn't apply to you! It's all about you!

Read Proverbs 1:1-7.
Answer these questions:

- What is the purpose of the proverbs? (See verses 2-6.)

- When you hear or see the word "righteousness," what images come to mind? Draw your ideas in the space below, if you'd like.

- How would you explain justice to a young child?

- What does it mean to have integrity? Explain.

- What is the beginning of knowledge?

- What does "fear of the Lord" mean to you? Do you fear the Lord? Why or why not?

- According to the verses, who despises wisdom and instruction?

- What was your favorite verse in this passage? Why?

GOING DEEPER:

- Do you respect God enough to desire what He wants for you, or do you think that His plans are just a far-off idea that you'll figure out when you're older? Explain.

- How might getting to know Him help you face tough decisions?

- Do you ever struggle to understand and believe that God really does care about you? Why? When?

- Are you willing to learn from His Word by spending time in it regularly? Why or why not?

day 3

Why should I want wisdom?

Wisdom sounds like something that your grandmother has, right? She's lived long enough to know a lot and always seems to know what to do.

Do you ever wish you knew what to do, too? Wisdom isn't just being smart; it's having knowledge and applying it to the situation. It's knowing God's Word and applying it to your life. Proverbs 2 contains a lot of reasons you should desire wisdom.

Read Proverbs 2 and Proverbs 3:13-26.
Answer these questions:

- In these verses, what is the relationship between the person speaking and the person listening? (See Prov. 2:1.)

- Is wisdom always easy to receive? Why or why not?

- Where does wisdom come from? (See Prov. 2:6.)

- From what things does the father tell his son that wisdom can rescue him? (See Prov. 2:10-19.)

- What two things does wisdom bring with it to watch over you? (See Prov. 2:11.) Have you ever experienced this in your own life? Explain.

- Use a pen, pencil, or makers, and draw all the ways wisdom is personified as a woman in Proverbs 3:13-18.

GOING DEEPER:

- Where could you use a little wisdom in your life right now? Close your eyes and think about it, then write about those situations.

- What situations stress you out? Why?

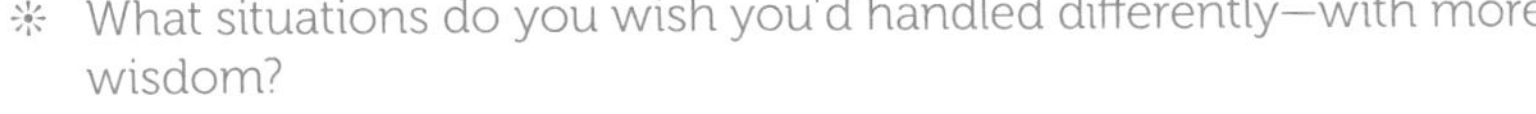

- What situations do you wish you'd handled differently—with more wisdom?

WAIT!

You're not quite done with today's study in Proverbs. Take a few minutes to look over the list of situations and areas in which you need wisdom that you just journaled about on the previous page. Then, pray about those situations. Maybe you pray best with your eyes closed. Perhaps you prefer to journal your prayers. It could be that you like to draw while you pray, or even pray or write Scripture verses that fit the situations you're currently facing. Spend some time doing just that today. Use this page to write, draw, or record your prayer.

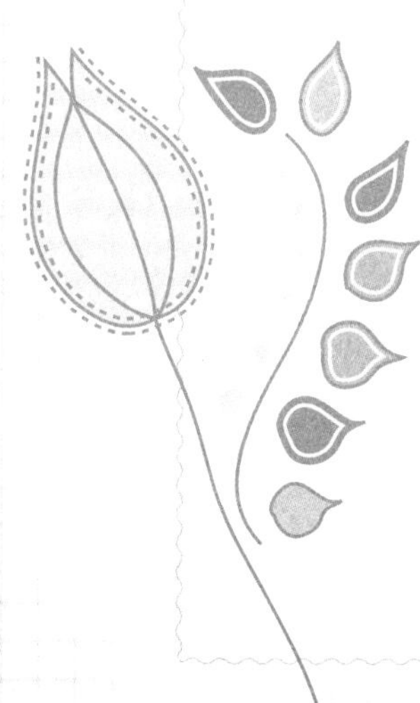

day 4

Asking for wisdom

Solomon was the wisest man who ever lived. He became wise (and you can, too!) by asking God for wisdom. God was so pleased with Solomon's request that He blessed him beyond what he'd asked.

Read 1 Kings 3, paying close attention to verses 3-14.

- Imagine you could ask God for anything. What would you ask for? Draw it below.

- How do you think Solomon was feeling when he asked God for wisdom? **(See verses 7-9.)**

- Why do you think God was pleased with Solomon's request?

- In verse 28, how did the people respond to Solomon's God-given wisdom?

- Has wisdom in action ever not made sense to you? When? Check out 1 Corinthians 2:14 for more on wisdom that may not make sense to the world. Record your thoughts, including questions, below. Ask God for wisdom in understanding and living according to His Word.

GOING DEEPER:

- Have you asked God for wisdom like Solomon did? Why or why not? If so, what happened? What did you learn?

- How would your life be different if you used your God-given wisdom more often? Explain.

- Read James 1:5-8. Remember it from this week's introduction? How do these verses say God will give wisdom to you? What must you not do in order to receive wisdom? Spend some time asking God for wisdom now. Be specific about the areas of your life in which you need God's wisdom most.

day 5

Living wisely by recognizing rebellion and repenting

We're all sinners. Big time. We've been that way since the day we were born. (Pay attention to verse 5 when you read Psalm 51!) Whether it's talking badly about some girl behind her back, having sex with your boyfriend, obsessing over your body and how it looks, cussing, or putting down your friends, we sin every day. Multiple times a day, in fact. That sin keeps us from seeing things and doing things God's way.

Read Psalm 51, then answer these questions:

- Which verse or verses speak to you the most in this passage? Why?

- Rewrite that verse (or verses) below in your own words.

- What does it mean to be rebellious? In what area(s) of your life are you rebellious? Explain.

- What are you feeling guilty about? Why?

- What does God desire in us? (See v. 17.) What does that mean? Explain.

- What does God teach us? **(See v. 6b.)** How has God taught you wisdom, even in the aftermath of sin?

GOING DEEPER:

Confess your sins to God. Start by asking the Holy Spirit to reveal any areas of sin in your life. When He does, admit them to God. Take responsibility, ask His forgiveness, and for His help in turning away from those things. Write them down, say them out loud—just get them out.

- Read verse 10 aloud. Repeat it to God as a prayer. If you'd like, write it below.

- What should the result of your confession be? (See Psalm 51:12-15.) Are you joyful, teaching others, and singing and praising God? What would that actually look like in your life? List some practical ideas for how you could live out that Scripture.

day 6

Walking wisely

Wisdom isn't just something you should tap into when making big decisions. It should affect how you treat each situation you come across every day: how you treat your mom when she's mad at you for being late; how you talk to your younger sibling when you really want to punch him or her in the face; how you speak in class when your beliefs are being attacked. Walking through each day with wisdom glorifies God and points others to Him. So, how can you walk wisely today (and every day)?

Read Ephesians 5:15-16 and Colossians 4:5.

- Are you paying attention to how you "walk"? Why or why not?

- What parts of your "walk" need attention right now? Why?

- Do you make the most of your time? How?

- How do you treat non-believers? Would they recognize you as a Christian? Are you different from them? Explain.

- What about the days you're living in makes them seem evil?

- How could you walk more wisely? List some practical ideas for how to make wise choices in situations you will face today.

GOING DEEPER:

- Hold out your hand and look at it. For each finger, come up with a way that you will make the most of your time today to make an impact for Christ. That's living wisely! List those five ways below. (One of them can be doing this quiet time and spending time with Him.) Then, actually **do** those things.

- 1.
- 2.
- 3.
- 4.
- 5.

day 7

A day for reflection

Read the following Scriptures and journal about them, explaining to God what you have learned about wisdom in these verses and how you can apply this Scripture to your daily life.

- James 1:5-8

- James 3:17

- Luke 2:52 (the only verse that tells us what Jesus was up to in His teen years)

The heart of her husband trusts in her, and he will not lack anything good. She rewards him with good, not evil, all the days of her life.

—Proverbs 31:11-12

week 2
being trustworthy

INTRODUCTION TO WEEK 2

Most people will let you down. It's easy to get your hopes up that some guy is going to come through and pull off the sweet surprise you were hoping for, but most of the time, guys fall short. And it's not just guys. Best friends might betray you; parents might not understand you.

You're not the first one who's felt frustrated with the lack of trustworthy people around her. A psalmist wrote about this thousands of years ago.

> "Those who know Your name trust in You because You have not abandoned those who seek You, Yahweh."
> —Psalm 9:10

The psalmist was remembering an experience in which he was dealing with an enemy and things seemed pretty hopeless. But God worked then, and He's still working today. He is trustworthy, and He is not going to break your trust. He is good because He is love. That is His essence, and it won't change. Now, He may not always act according to your timetable or your plan. This is a hard fact to accept about God. He doesn't seem to be concerned about meeting our needs as quickly as we'd like Him to at times. But this is an opportunity for you to walk down the two-way street of trust and extend Him yours. Tell Him that you trust His provision and His timing. He'll prove His trustworthiness in time.

And you'll have plenty of opportunities to prove yours.

THIS WEEK'S THEME

This week your study of Proverbs 31 will focus on **trustworthiness**. It's easy to see that trustworthiness is important to God. As Psalm 9:10 points out, trustworthiness is one of God's characteristics.

In fact, Psalm 9:10 isn't the only place that attests to God's trustworthiness. In Hebrews 13:5-6, we're told that God Himself has said He will never leave or forsake us, which encourages us to live without fear, knowing God can be trusted to do what He has said He will do. Psalms is full of testimonies of God's faithfulness. In Psalm 3:5, God is the One who sustains us. In Psalm 5:11, He is a trustworthy shelter who causes the people who trust Him to rejoice. The psalmist invites readers to commit their ways to the Lord and trust Him, with the assurance that God will act (Psalm 37:5). In times of fear, we're encouraged to place our trust in God and His Word (Psalm 56).

Even Proverbs has something to say about God's trustworthiness. Fear is a trap according to Proverbs 29:25, but the person who trusts in God will be protected. Check out Proverbs 3:5-6. What does it say?

> "Trust in the LORD with all your heart, and do not rely on your own understanding; think about Him in all your ways, and He will guide you on the right paths."
> —Proverbs 3:5-6

Clearly, God is trustworthy. We can trust Him to do what He has said He will do. His Word is true and reliable, and when we trust in Him, He promises to guide us along right paths. But what about you? Are you a trustworthy person?

FIRST THINGS FIRST

Remember last week when you read Proverbs 31 beginning with verse 10? Do it again, focusing on verses 11 and 12. What important idea do you find in these verses?

That's right, trustworthiness. The godly woman described in Proverbs 31 was trustworthy, and her trustworthiness had an effect on the people around her. If trustworthiness is one of God's characteristics and one of the qualities listed in the Proverbs 31 description of a godly woman, then trustworthiness must be pretty important to God.

That's why it should be important to us, too.

So, how can we be trustworthy? Being trustworthy requires a determination to maintain a confidence (Prov. 11:13) and not gossip. It involves controlling your tongue so that you don't lie or deceive others (Ps. 34:13; Prov. 12:19). It means you do what you say you will, follow through on your commitments, and keep your promises.

So, how trustworthy are you, really? Let's dig in to Proverbs 31 and find out!

day 1

A trustworthy woman

I hope you have a new understanding of the importance of wisdom from last week. This week, we're going to talk about trust and being trustworthy.

Read Proverbs 31:11-12, then answer these questions.

- What exactly is trust, and why is it so important?

- How important is it that you trust your best friend?

- Do you think girls or guys are more trustworthy? Explain.

- Why is it key for guys to see that a girl is trustworthy?

✳ In what ways do you prove that you are not trustworthy?

✳ Why might showing that you're not trustworthy keep a guy from wanting to be around you?

There are two parts to the trust we're studying in these verses: the husband's part and the wife's part. Although you're not married, it's still important to understand that **trust is a two-way street.** It has to be given (or proven) by one party, and it has to be accepted by the other in a healthy relationship. Verse 11 says "the heart of her husband trusts in her." Other translations say that "her husband has full confidence in her."

✳ How many guys do you know who open up about what's going on in their hearts?

✳ Why do you think it's hard for guys to discuss how they're feeling?

✳ Why do you think this particular husband was able to trust his wife?

✳ Check the last part of verse 11 and all of verse 12 for the answer: he doesn't lack anything good; she rewards him with good things! What kind of good things can you think of that might happen in a marriage that would cause a man to feel rewarded?

WEEKLY MEMORY VERSE:

"A gossip goes around revealing a secret, but the trustworthy keeps a confidence."
—Proverbs 11:13

GOING DEEPER:

What are some things you can do this week to be a trustworthy young woman? Think about the following scenarios and write out an action plan for how to be trustworthy in each situation.

- You have a friend who constantly gossips.
- You are tempted to lie to your teacher when she asked if you did your own homework because you know you just copied someone else's.

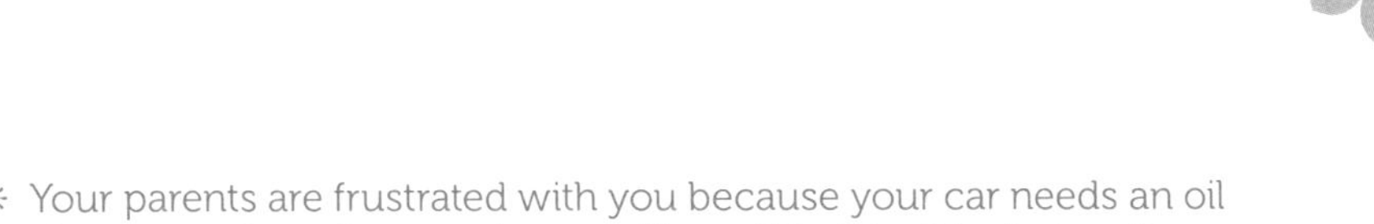

- Your parents are frustrated with you because your car needs an oil change, and you keep saying you "forgot" to take it in, but really you just didn't take it in because there was something more fun going on after school.

Think about the week you have ahead of you. What are some practical choices you can make today to be trustworthy in these areas:

- With your family?
- At school?
- With your friends?
- When you're alone?
- Online?

day 2

Is anyone trustworthy?

It's hard to find a person on this earth whom you can trust all the time. But God can be trusted. Sure, His timetable is a little different than ours, but you can trust that He is always working things out for His good purposes.

Read Psalm 19:7; 33:4; 111:7. Answer these questions:

- What do these verses say about God's instruction (or law)?

- What do these verses say about God's testimony (or statutes)?

- What do these verses teach you about God's Word?

- What are the works of God's hands? Close your eyes and picture as many as you can in one minute. List or draw some of them in the space provided.

- Look over Psalm 111:7 again. Do you see truth and justice in your life? Where? Explain.

- Do you trust God? Why or why not? How do these verses challenge or support your stance?

GOING DEEPER:

- Tell God why you might have a hard time trusting Him. Write it. Draw it. Speak it out loud. Just talk to Him about it!

- Have you seen God work in a situation that proved His faithfulness? If so, write out your praises to Him for it. If not, ask Him to work in a situation where you need to see His faithfulness.

- Take a sip of your latte, soda, or whatever you're sipping on right now. Really taste its flavor. (If you're drinking water, notice its temperature and texture.) How does the command in Psalm 34:8 to "Taste and see that the Lord is good" relate? If you can't actually taste the Lord's goodness, then what did the psalmist mean? When have you experienced God's goodness?

- To savor something means to enjoy it completely and dwell on it. How does that apply to God's trustworthiness? How can you savor the Lord's goodness and trustworthiness in your life today? List some practical ideas.

day 3

What happens if I put my trust in the Lord?

There are a lot of people who want your trust: car salesmen, politicians, doctors, friends, and the people on infomercials. Some of them deserve our trust, and some of them don't. Trust is a two-way street, and trusting God is no different. He will prove Himself trustworthy to you. Will you prove yourself trustworthy to Him?

Read Psalm 40:1-5. Answer these questions:

- How did the psalmist wait for the Lord?
- Are you a patient or impatient person? Why?
- Look over verse 3. What is the song in your mouth? Does it need to be replaced? Why or why not?
- Why are you tempted to run to the proud (or the popular people) or those who run after lies (which means they chase things the world says are important, like making a lot of money, wearing designer clothes, having perfect skin, etc.)? Explain.
- According to these verses, what happens to you when you put your trust in the Lord? How have you seen God work in your life when you've trusted Him?
- Verse 5 says that God has done many wonderful things. What wonderful things has He done for you?

GOING DEEPER:

- In what situation(s) are you waiting patiently for the Lord to work? What have you learned about trusting Him in these situations?

- Waiting for God isn't easy. Journal about the situation(s) you listed above, how tough it is to wait, and how ready you are for Him to prove Himself trustworthy.

- Tap into your creative side. In the space below, paint, draw, or write about God's wonderful works and plans for your life.

day 4

Case in point: A trustworthy man

Daniel is one of my favorite Bible characters. I love how he remained faithful through multiple trials, never doubting that the Lord was sovereign and His plan was trustworthy. He proved his own trustworthiness, not only to God, but also to everyone who encountered him in Babylon.

Read Daniel 6.

- Why did the men not like Daniel?

- How did Daniel prove himself trustworthy to God?

- How did God prove Himself trustworthy to Daniel?

- How did King Darius react to what he saw the morning after he put Daniel in the lions' den?

- What happened to the backbiting, gossiping, plotting men who tried to trap Daniel?

GOING DEEPER:

- Has anyone ever plotted against you? If so, journal about how that felt. How did God prove Himself trustworthy in that situation?

- How tempting was it to respond to plots against you with a plot for revenge? Did you? Why or why not?

- Write out a prayer to God below, asking for the willpower to trust Him in a situation you're facing, even if it feels like you've been thrown in a lions' den. Also, tell Him how you feel about that situation, including your thoughts about the people who have plotted against you. Be honest!

day 5

When no one else seems trustworthy

Ever feel like you can only trust yourself? You're not alone. As females, it's easy to feel the pressure to betray a confidence, gossip, or break a promise. You're extremely blessed if you haven't had someone share your secrets, gossip about you, or break a promise to you. People have been dealing with folks they couldn't trust since time began. The psalmist knew exactly what you're going through.

Read all of Psalm 56, then Psalm 118:8.

- Can you relate to the psalmist feeling pursued and attacked? Why?

- Does anyone come to mind when you read Psalm 56:5-6? Of what do you need to forgive that person? What steps will you take to do so today?

- What should be your remedy when you feel like everyone's against you? (See Ps. 56:3-4.)

- Taking refuge means you are safe from pursuit or danger. What does it mean to take refuge in God? Explain.

- Memorize Psalm 118:8. Have you ever taken refuge in God? Why?

GOING DEEPER:

- Is there someone you trust who doesn't deserve your trust? Explain.

- What would be the wise thing to do in the situation you described above? Spend some time praying about the situation and write down what God reveals to you.

- Is there someone trusting you whose trust you know you don't deserve? Explain. Why don't you deserve that person's trust? Do you need to be honest with him or her or ask for forgiveness? What is the right thing for you to do in this situation? What steps will you take to do that today?

day 6

Being trustworthy yourself

Are you the one people come to when they want to know the latest gossip? Has something you've said ever gotten you in trouble?

Most of us run our mouths more than we should. Something about being in the know makes girls feel so good. But when our lips are moving, we have to be certain that the words coming out of our mouths are pleasing to God. Why? So that we can show that we're trustworthy with information that's been given to us. And sometimes that means we have to keep our mouths shut.

But being trustworthy is about more than what comes out of our mouths; it has everything to do with our actions as well.

Read Proverbs 17:17; 18:24; 27:6,9.

- In Proverbs 17:17, we read that a friend loves at all times. Do you have that kind of friend? Are you that kind of friend? Explain.

- In Proverbs 18:24, we read about a friend who sticks closer than a brother. How is your relationship with your sibling(s)? Are you closer to your friend(s) or your sibling(s)? Explain.

- How can you show both your sibling(s) and your friend(s) how grateful you are for them? List some practical ideas below.

- Proverbs 27:6 tells us that the wounds of a friend are trustworthy. Has a friend ever told you something true about yourself but it still hurt? Were you eventually grateful for his or her honesty? Why or why not?

- Look at Proverbs 27:9. Do you have friends who are good at giving advice? Is their advice trustworthy? Why or why not?

- Do you give good advice? Why or why not?

GOING DEEPER:

- In what situations or specific relationships do you need to prove your trustworthiness? Think about situations within your family, at school, even in your relationships with friends or boyfriends. (Keep in mind that this a long-term process.)

- What steps will you take today to show that you are trustworthy in those situations or relationships?

- Is there a person who has the wrong impression of you, specifically when it comes to being trustworthy? What will you do today to begin to change his or her perception of you?

day 7

A day for reflection

Read the following Scriptures and write about each one, explaining to God how these verses challenged you to live differently:

- Proverbs 11:13

- Isaiah 12:2

- Isaiah 40:31

> She selects wool and flax and works with willing hands. She is like the merchant ships, bringing her food from far away. She rises while it is still night and provides food for her household and portions for her female servants . . . She watches over the activities of her household and is never idle.
>
> —Proverbs 31:13-15,27

week 3
buckle down

INTRODUCTION TO WEEK 3

Remember that group project when So-and-So didn't pull her weight? Do you recall the frustration of dealing with someone who simply didn't take any pride in her work or put in any effort to do a good job on the project? So, in addition to your own assignments, you and the other team members had to take care of the things your lazy group member let slip through the cracks.

Frustrating, wasn't it?

But hopefully, that experience taught you that there's something to be said for hard work and doing a job well. Laziness and a bad attitude simply don't lead to a job well done. Scripture has a few things to say about how we work. Check out Proverbs 18:9. What does it say?

> "The one who is truly lazy in his work is brother to a vandal."
> —Proverbs 18:9

Clearly, God expects those who follow Him to be hard-working and diligent in their work. If you're a diligent worker, then you take a certain amount of pride in your work. You don't do it half-heartedly or just slap something together to meet a deadline. A diligent worker is conscientious about her work, making an effort to guard against laziness and fully concentrate on the task at hand. As believers, that's how we're called to work.

Doing a job right is only part of it. Doing it with the right attitude is the other. Sure, things can get done without a smile on your face or joy in your heart. But that's not how we're called to work. Paul tells us in 1 Corinthians 10:31, "Whatever you do, do everything for God's glory." Colossians 3:23 encourages us to do our work with enthusiasm, "as something done for the Lord and not for men." And in Philippians 2:14, he tells us to do "everything without grumbling or arguing."

How much time and energy might you have saved by doing the task assigned to you without complaining? God has made you capable of great things, but how diligent are you in completing the work involved?

THIS WEEK'S THEME

This week, your study of Proverbs 31 will focus on **diligence**, with emphasis on Proverbs 31:13-15,27. Read those verses right now.

In these verses, the capable woman we've been studying is described as a hard worker—and she works willingly. She isn't lazy, idle, or solely focused on her own needs. She's diligent in her work, pays attention to details, and loves variety. She embodies the godly attitude toward work found in Ephesians 4:28 and 1 Thessalonians 4:11-12. Read them now.

> "The thief must no longer steal. Instead, he must do honest work with his own hands, so that he has something to share with anyone in need."
> —Ephesians 4:28

". . .seek to lead a quiet life, to mind your own business, and to work with your own hands, as we commanded you, so that you may walk properly in the presence of outsiders and not be dependent on anyone."
—1 Thessalonians 4:11-12

As believers, we are to do honest work. Laziness, deception, and unethical behavior shouldn't characterize our lives or our work ethic. According to these verses, the way we do our work should provide for our needs and allow us to help others in need. In addition, our work should help us to "walk properly in the presence of outsiders," meaning that we shouldn't be involved in anything that casts a bad light on Christ, is immoral, or is unethical.

The woman in Proverbs 31 valued hard work and was diligent in it. You are a Proverbs 31 girl. How diligent are you? It's time to find out!

day 1
A hard-workin' woman

Our capable woman isn't a spoiled woman. She doesn't sit around all day, playing on her phone, watching TV, and ordering around servants. Oh no, the ideal woman is a hard worker.

Read Proverbs 31:13-15,27, then answer these questions.

- Who's the hardest worker you know?
- What keeps this person focused on his or her task?
- What does the last part of verse 13 say? Why is the fact that she was willing to work important?
- How often are you willing to work hard? Explain.

※ Do you ever take pleasure in your work? Why or why not?

Proverbs 31:14 tells us that the woman is like the merchant ships, bringing her food in from far away. This lady doesn't just grow her own food. She trades what she grows for foods brought in from other lands. She likes variety! Do you? Or are you stuck in rut—food, clothing, or entertainment-wise?

※ What's your favorite food?

※ How often do you eat it?

※ Do you have a favorite shirt or pair of jeans?

※ How often do you wear them?

※ Do you find yourself wearing the same thing over and over? Why?

※ Do you listen to the same kind of music all the time? Why?

Life is not meant to be boring! God gave us a beautiful planet and tons of different foods to enjoy. Music, food, clothing—all these things add variety to our lives and can be used to celebrate this life He gave us to LIVE! (See John 10:10b—*"I have come so that they may have life and have it in abundance."*)

※ Are you living abundantly? Why or why not?

※ What new food will you try this week?

※ What new types of music will you listen to this week?

※ What new way will you connect with God this week?

Look at verses 15 and 27, then answer the following questions:

- Why did this woman get up so early? What was she doing?
- What can you infer about her since she made sure her servants were fed?
- Why do you think verse 27 says she was never idle?

GOING DEEPER:

So, what can we learn from these verses? First of all, laziness is not a characteristic of this woman. She gets up early and works hard. There's a lot to do, so she doesn't have time for idleness. And apparently, she's caring, if she's making sure that both her family and her servants are fed. She looks out for others, which is a trait of hers that we'll study more in depth later. How do you compare to her? Let's find out! Answer these questions:

- How early do you wake up?
- What do you do once you get out of bed?
- What are you thinking about in the morning? Are you only thinking about your own needs or those of others?
Why or why not?

WEEKLY MEMORY VERSE:

"Do everything without grumbling and arguing, so that you may be blameless and pure, children of God who are faultless in a crooked and perverted generation, among whom you shine like stars in the world."
—Philippians 2:14-15

* Do you ever find yourself bored, without anything to do? How could you use that time to glorify God and help others? List some practical ideas below.

This week we learned that our protagonist is a hard worker who gets up early and brings variety to her life and the lives of those around her. I get the feeling that she's capable, confident, and loving. What do you think about her?

* What do you like best about her so far?

* How are you striving to be like her?

day 2
The value of work

Work (be it school work or a job) is part of God's plan for us. Adam and Eve were given the job of tending the Garden of Eden even before they sinned. Work is one way we find fulfillment, and it's also a means of providing for ourselves.

Read Proverbs 12:14 and 14:23. Answer these questions:

* How does Proverbs 12:14 tie together last week's lesson (about being trustworthy in our words and actions) and this week's?

- Has the work of your hands ever rewarded you? How?

- What does Proverbs 14:23 tell us there is in hard work? What does that mean? What does it look like in your life?

- What does endless talk lead to, according to Proverbs 14:23?

- In what areas of your life are you all talk? Explain.

- How does talking keep you from doing what God has called you to do?

GOING DEEPER:

- What's your attitude toward work? Why do you feel that way? Does your attitude match up with God's? Why or why not? What changes will you make today so that it does?

- What task, chore, or assignment is stressing you out right now? Why?

- Now that you're all stressed out after the last question, take five deep breaths. Invite God into your stress and **ask God to help you complete the stressful task, chore, or assignment that you are facing**. Write a prayer below, telling Him all about why you're stressed.

- What task do you need to tackle today without grumbling or complaining, as Philippians 2:14 says?

day 3

Why we work

Like we've discussed before, we're on earth to glorify God. Everything we do should reflect God's goodness and character. Our work is one way we can show others how He's changing us because ultimately, leading them to know Christ is the work we're supposed to be accomplishing.

Read 1 Corinthians 15:58, then answer these questions:

- In what ways are you steadfast **(standing firm)**? Explain.

- In what areas of your life do you need to be a little more dedicated and constant? Why?

- When have you felt like your work was in vain? Why did you feel that way?

- Have you ever been on a mission trip or service project where you felt like you weren't successful? Describe that time.

- Are you excelling in the Lord's work, or are you even aware that He has things for you to do? Explain.

※ What comfort do you get from this verse?

※ What difficult tasks do you know God has called you to. How will you depend on God's strength to get you through those tasks?

GOING DEEPER:

Put your pen or pencil down. Now, take a few minutes to dream. If you could serve God and His kingdom in any way, what would it be? Don't think about the roadblocks to serving Him in that way. Just dream.

※ What ideas came to your mind? List or draw them below.

※ Take some time to write out a prayer to God, asking Him to open your eyes to ways you can put those ideas to work for His kingdom. Pray for His leadership in your life and ask Him to make His dreams become your dreams. Go ahead and express your confidence that He can do this things. After all, all things are possible with God (Mark 10:27)!

day 4

Doing what you're asked

Sometimes being told to do something makes us mad. We just don't like being told what to do all the time! And sometimes we don't follow through with what we've been told to do. Jesus told a story that illustrates this.

Read Matthew 21:28-31a.

- What did the first son say?
- What did he ultimately end up doing?
- What do you think made him change his mind?
- What did the second son say and do?
- In both cases, the sons' responses to their father didn't match their actions. Why did Jesus say that the first son did his father's will?

- What would the ideal response from either son have been?

- How does this story portray the truth that our actions speak louder than our words?

GOING DEEPER:

- Which son in the parable are you more like? Why?

- Is there something you've been asked to do that you need to follow through with? What is it? Write about it below.

* Come up with an action plan below, outlining the steps you'll take, starting today, to follow through with the task you listed in the previous question. Doing what you said you would do honors God.

* Admit to God the times that you haven't followed through by writing a prayer of confession below.

day 5

Passing the test

Do you ever get nervous when you know you're being evaluated? Giving a speech, knowing that your test is on the teacher's desk being graded, or enduring a sports tryout—all of these can be nerve-wracking experiences because your performance determines the outcome. Your efforts will be judged, and the results can be good or bad. Similarly, our lives are being evaluated by God, and the quality of our work will be judged.

Read 1 Corinthians 3:5-15, then answer these questions:

* According to 1 Corinthians 3:13, how will our work be tested?

- Has your work ever been tested before? What happened? Explain.

- We're called God's coworkers in this passage. What does that mean? What does it look like in real life?

- What kind of "work" was Paul referring to in this passage?

- Do you ever compare your work to others? Why or why not?

Read Galatians 6:4.

- What does Galatians 6:4 have to say about comparing your work to others?

- Is this a big issue for you? Why or why not?

GOING DEEPER:

- What changes do you need to make to your work ethic, knowing that how you work is so important to God? Make an action plan for how you'll do so, starting today.

- Picture what would happen if a fire started in your room. Clothes destroyed, priceless pictures turned to ashes, expensive electronics melted and smoking. It's hard to survive a fire. Based on 1 Corinthians 3:13, how do you think the quality of your work for God's kingdom will hold up when it's tested by fire? Explain. Use drawings, words, poetry, or whatever best allows you to get your thoughts out on this page.

day 6

Not because others are looking

Let's be honest. It's a lot harder to be diligent when no one's watching. We cut ourselves some slack when the teacher's out of the room or when our boss is away from work. But that's not the way Christ wants us to work.

Read Ephesians 6:6-8, then answer these questions:

- Why does verse 6 say we might work only while we're being watched? Do you do that? Explain.

- Why should you not be concerned with pleasing men (or those who are watching us)?

- How are believers labeled in verse 6? What does it mean to be a "slave" of Christ? How will you submit yourself to Jesus' authority today at school? With your parents? With your friends? At practice?

- According to verse 7, how should you serve? Do you? What would help you have a better attitude toward service?

GOING DEEPER:

- Serving others isn't easy. List some times when you've had to swallow your pride and serve others. What happened? What did God teach you?

- Working hard isn't easy either. List some times when you haven't worked diligently because no one was looking.

- OK, now celebrate your hard work for a minute. When have you worked diligently even though no one was looking? How was your work pleasing to God?

- What about God and His Son makes you want to work with excellence at all times? Why?

day 7
A day for reflection

Read the following Scriptures and write a sentence or two about each one, explaining to God how these verses have challenged the way you work:

- Proverbs 13:4

- Proverbs 21:5

- 2 Timothy 2:15

She evaluates a field and buys it;
she plants a vineyard with her earnings. She draws
on her strength and reveals that her arms are strong.
She sees that her profits are good, and her lamp never
goes out at night. She extends her hands to the spinning
staff, and her hands hold the spindle . . . She makes her
own bed coverings; her clothing is fine linen and purple.
. . . She makes and sells linen garments; she delivers
belts to the merchants.

—Proverbs 31:16-19,22,24

week 4

smart and strong

INTRODUCTION TO WEEK 4

Have you ever acted dumb to impress a guy or to fit in? For some reason, around middle school, we girls get the idea that not knowing the answer (or at least pretending not to know it) is cool. Why do you think that is? Write your thoughts below.

God's Word, on the other hand, never asks us to pretend to be anything we're not. In fact, Scripture says we're pretty remarkable. Don't believe it? Read Psalm 139:14. Then read it again, aloud this time.

> "I will praise You because I have been remarkably and wonderfully made. Your works are wonderful, and I know this very well." —Psalm 139:14

You are "remarkably and wonderfully made," which means you don't need to pretend you're anything you're not. You don't have to disguise your intelligence just to impress a guy or make him feel important. In fact, when you do so, you're hiding one of the very remarkable things about yourself that God intended to shine.

Think about the well-known godly women highlighted in Scripture. They didn't hide their intelligence; they used it! Rahab was a prostitute, but she was also a smart woman of great faith whose quick thinking and obedience saved the lives of the Israelite spies and those of her own family. Ruth was a foreign woman in a strange land, but she didn't let that stop her from finding a way to provide grain for herself and Naomi. When she was obedient to Naomi's wise instructions, she became the wife of Boaz, and an important person in the lineage of Christ. Check it all out in the Book of Ruth. There's the beautiful, intelligent, and courageous Esther who saved her people from destruction (Esther 2–10); Deborah, the wise and humble judge of Israel (Judges 4-5); and Mary, the mother of Christ, who pondered God's words in her heart and trusted Him, even when what the angel said seemed impossible.

Women of God are smart, strong, faithful and true. Need more proof? Check out the capable woman of Proverbs 31 we've been studying.

THIS WEEK'S THEME

Smart and strong is a good description of the Proverbs 31 woman. This week's study will focus on Proverbs 31:16-19,22,24. In those verses, our new friend is looking at land, evaluating it, then buying the field. She's planting crops, making clothes and bedspreads, and conducting business—and there are even a few verses that endlessly detail her strong arms. She's clearly intelligent—and not afraid to use her brain!

What does verse 18 say?

"She sees that her profits are good, and her lamp never goes out at night." —Proverbs 31:18

This lady kept up with her finances and knew how much money she was making. Interpretations differ on how to take "her lamp never goes out at night." It could be taken to mean that she stayed up late, tending to all she had to do. It could also mean that she was conscientious enough to be aware of how much oil was in her lamp and to keep it filled. Either way, we get the idea that this lady's life wasn't out of control.

Today we can apply verse 18 to our lives by making sure that we are responsible stewards of God's money and time. Tithing, saving, and spending money responsibly are all important habits for godly women to have.

Something to think about: Are you tithing? (To tithe is to give a tenth of your income to the church for God's use.)

Giving God a portion of the money you get (be it paychecks, gifts, allowances, etc.) shows your love for Him, enables other people to benefit, and allows God to bless you even more. See Malachi 3:10. It isn't easy to tithe, especially when money's tight and there's something you really want. But it's important.

A godly woman is obedient. She's trustworthy and diligent in her work, as we've previously studied. But she's also smart and strong, and doesn't try to hide it.

Do you? Embrace your strength and intelligence this week as we dive deeper into Proverbs 31!

day 1

Smart and strong

You'll see that our capable woman in Proverbs 31 didn't mess around when it came to her intelligence.

Read Proverbs 31:16-19,22,24. Clearly, this woman is a thinker. She analyzed the potential purchase and thought about the decision. Apparently, she's good at making decisions because previous purchases or endeavors have given her "earnings." She's a wise businesswoman.

- What about you? What was the last thing you bought?

- How long did you consider the purchase before you made it?

- Is that typically how you buy things? Explain.

⁜ Are you usually satisfied with your purchases, or do you end up returning or not using the majority of things you buy?

⁜ What did the Proverbs 31 woman decide to do with the field she bought?

⁜ What does verse 17 tell us about her?

That's right . . . she's strong. She's got muscular arms. We discussed last week that the Proverbs 31 woman was not a spoiled lady who sat around all day and snacked, texted, and watched TV. She worked. And since they didn't have gyms or weightlifting equipment back then, we can be pretty sure that she was doing some heavy lifting to develop those strong arms.

⁜ What about you? Do you take care of yourself physically?

⁜ Do you eat right? Why or why not?

⁜ Do you exercise a few times a week?

⁜ Do you get enough sleep? Why or why not?

⁜ How is taking care of yourself pleasing to God?

✻ What will you do this week to take better care of yourself? List some practical steps you will take to do so.

GOING DEEPER:

Read Proverbs 31:19,22,24, which give us a few more clues as to what the Proverbs 31 woman made. In addition to the clothes she made for her family, she also made bed coverings, fine clothes for herself, and enough extra clothing to be taken to the merchants to sell for a profit. Once again, we see her diligence and her business sense.

God has blessed you with a brain that He'd like you to use. If He's given you arms and legs that work, He wants you to use them. You have unique skills God has given you.

✻ Can you speak intelligently, do well on a test, or perform well in a sport and give Him credit for it? Why or why not?

✻ In what areas of your life are you hiding or not using the intelligence, strength, or skills God gave you? Write an action plan for how you can start exercising those gifts for His glory this week.

WEEKLY MEMORY VERSE:

"So we must not get tired of doing good, for we will reap at the proper time if we don't give up."
—Galatians 6:9

- Where are some places where you can work, serve, and give Him glory? Ask God to open your eyes to the opportunities He is already providing for you to do so. Write your prayer and list the opportunities in the space below. Be obedient to follow through and get involved in the ways He leads you to.

day 2

Because He said so

Work isn't an option. I hate to break it you, but if you're alive, you're not supposed to be idle. Not that you'll necessarily get paid for all of your work, but being lazy isn't part of God's plan. (Check out Proverbs for lots of verses on laziness.) But God doesn't expect us to slave our lives away. He knows that we need rest. Purposeful rest is important, and it honors God.

Read Exodus 20:8-11. Answer these questions:

- Whose example are we to follow by resting one day a week?

- How many days did God command us to work in a week?

- How many days a week do most people work today?

- Do you take time to really rest on Sunday? Why or why not?

- Do you take time to rest at some other time during the week? Why or why not?

❊ What evidence do you see in your life that you need to rest?

❊ Why do you think God wants us to rest?

GOING DEEPER:

On the continuum below, mark the spot that represents how you do your work:

with complaining and grumbling ⟷ with persistence and dedication

❊ What does your answer tell you about yourself? What needs to change?

❊ Whatever type of "work" you do, be it physical labor, studying, homework, sports practice, etc., it is important to honor God with your work. Do you? How?

❊ What keeps you from resting? Explain.

- How will you make time so you can be committed to resting this week? What are some practical ideas for ways to rest that you can put into practice in your life this week? List them below.

day 3

The best-laid plans . . .

Have you ever attempted to plan an event at your school or church? What if you worked really hard, only to realize that you didn't have permission to have the event in the first place? All that work would be pointless. Similarly, if we don't have the Lord's approval on our plans, they won't succeed.

Read Psalm 127:1-2, then answer these questions:

- What does this passage say about hard work done without the Lord's approval?

- Have you ever worked hard at something that had the Lord's approval? If so, what was the outcome?

- Have you ever worked hard at something that did **not** have God's approval? If so, what happened? What did you learn?

- If we're called to work hard, then what does verse 2 mean? Why is working hard at something that doesn't have God's approval working in vain?

- Verse 2 says that God gives sleep to the one He loves. What does that mean?

GOING DEEPER:

- Describe a time when you've been frustrated because your hard work didn't pay off.

- What are some areas in your life where your plans and God's don't match up? List them here. Then spend some time praying over that list, asking God to line your heart up with His.

- Why do you think God wants you to make sure your purposes line up with His when you set out to do something?

⁜ How can you make sure your plans line up with God's?

day 4

Do your own work

Has anyone ever cheated off of you in school by borrowing answers to a homework assignment? Maybe she asked you to tell her what was on the test, or he didn't do his fair share of work in a group project. Did it make you mad? Why? Write about it below.

You did the work in order to know the answer or complete the project, and there they were, reaping the benefits of your efforts. Their actions showed a lack of integrity. But have you ever been the cheater?

If so, your actions reveal a lack of integrity.

Read 2 Thessalonians 3:10-13. Answer these questions:

⁜ Do you have some classmates who are irresponsible, idle, and interfere with the work of others? Explain.

⁜ Are you one of these classmates at times? Why?

⁜ How does Paul command those people to work?

- What's the benefit of such work? Explain.

- Scripture says the benefit is that they "eat their own bread," which means they are able to provide for themselves. For you as a student, what might be the equivalent?

Read Galatians 6:9. Answer these questions:

- What does it mean to grow weary in doing good?

- When have you grown weary in doing good? Explain.

- Why is it easy to get tired when you're doing good things?

GOING DEEPER:

- ❊ If you felt like Paul might have been referring to you when he talked about someone who doesn't work, but interferes in the work of others, what will you do differently this week?

- ❊ If you're one of the students who works hard and takes up slack for others, how do you find encouragement in Paul's command to not grow weary in doing good?

- ❊ What will you stop (or start) doing in order to encourage classmates/ siblings/coworkers to pull their own weight?

day 5

Shine on

What do your actions say about God? If you claim to follow Christ and yet you cheat in school, get drunk on the weekends, or goof off at your job, you cast a bad light on the name of Christ. We are to live in such a way that others want to know why we're different, why we do the right thing, why we work hard, and love other people when others don't.

Read Matthew 5:13-16. Answer these questions:

- ❊ What does it mean to be the salt of the earth and the light of the world?

- What does the way you live your life say to people who are watching you?

- What are some practical ways you can let your light shine today?

- Who is someone you know whose actions almost always point to Christ? In what way?

- How are you similar to that person?

- How are you different from that person?

- According to the last part of verse 16, what is the purpose of our good works?

GOING DEEPER:

- Carefully light a candle. Watch the flame flicker. If possible, turn out the lights in the room. As you look at the candle and how it illuminates the room, think about your actions. Think about how even small actions motivated by God's love will point others to His light. Do you shine a light that points people in a dark world toward God? Why or why not?

- If after evaluating your life you don't think your light is shining very brightly in the world, what practical changes will you make this week to fan the flame?

- Our works are supposed to glorify God, not ourselves. But sometimes it's easy to get caught up in doing the right thing because it makes us feel good, elevates our status, or gets us attention. What can you do to deflect the praise you may get for the good things you do to the One who truly deserves it?

day 6

The whole point

We work hard to get ahead in school so we can eventually get good jobs. Then, we put in a lot of time and effort here on this earth earning money to make sure we can see the newest movie, buy the latest fashions, or have the newest technology.

Do you ever feel like the whole world is just spinning faster and faster, yet missing the point?

Read John 6:27; Mark 8:36; and 1 Corinthians 15:58. Answer these questions:

- We have to work. It's a given. But we can't forget that the "food" we're striving for is more than just literal food. Based on John 6:27, what do you think that "food" is?

- Are you striving for the food mentioned in John 6:27? Explain your answer.

- Mark 8:36 says that a man can work to gain the whole world, but still lose his life. Can you think of any people who have money, fame and success but are still lost with no hope for eternity?

- How have you tried to gain the whole world (or parts of it)? What is God's point of view on that?

- What do you think it's like to "labor in the Lord" as mentioned in 1 Corinthians 15:58? Why would work of that nature never be in vain?

GOING DEEPER:

- In your opinion, what is the purpose of life?

- Honestly evaluate. What would you say the purpose of your life was today or this week? **(Hint: look at where you've spent your time, money, thoughts, and words.)**

- Is there someone (including yourself) who needs to be reminded that success, good grades, and athletic success are not the primary purpose of life? What would God say to that person? How can you reach out to him or her today?

- How will this new perspective affect your life: friendships, spending habits, and your work ethic? List your ideas below as you pray for God to begin this work in you.

day 7

A day for reflection

Read the following Scriptures and write a sentence or two about each in your journal, explaining to God how these verses made an impact on you:

- Proverbs 12:14

- Proverbs 14:23

- 1 Corinthians 3:13-15

> She extends her hands to
> the spinning staff, and her
> hands hold the spindle.
> Her hands reach out to the
> poor, and she extends her
> hands to the needy.
>
> —Proverbs 31:19-20

week 5 love for others

INTRODUCTION TO WEEK 5

Think about someone you know who is in need right now. Maybe it's a girl at school whose family can't afford to meet her basic needs. Perhaps hungry children in another country came to mind. Maybe you thought about that homeless man on the corner, the tired woman who used food stamps in the line at the grocery store yesterday, or the family that will live in the Habitat for Humanity house that you worked on last week.

The fact remains that there are people in this world—and that includes your community, your school, and even your own family—who are in need. This world is filled with people who are hungry, tired, broken, deceived, destitute, addicted, and penniless. The question isn't if you're going to be faced with a person in need; it's when.

And you get to decide how you'll respond.

Will you reach out to the needy or will you ignore them? Is helping those in need your duty or someone else's problem?

Scripture isn't silent on the subject of how believers should respond to the needy in this world. Read 1 John 3:17. What does it say?

"If anyone has this world's goods and sees his brother in need but closes his eyes to his need—how can God's love reside in him?" —1 John 3:17

Now consider Luke 12:33. Does it shed any light on the subject?

"Sell your possessions and give to the poor. Make money-bags for yourselves that won't grow old, an inexhaustible treasure in heaven, where no thief comes near and no moth destroys." —Luke 12:33

As Christ-followers, we're clearly called to reach out to those in need. Our compassion toward those in need is a sign of God's presence in our lives (1 John 3:17) and tangible proof of God's love to a desperate world. And Luke 12:33 tells us that reaching out to the poor in God's name allows us to store up treasures for ourselves in heaven that we couldn't even begin to imagine if we tried.

INTRODUCTION TO THIS WEEK'S THEME

This week's study of the capable woman in Proverbs 31 will center on her **love for others.** Last week, verse 19 left us watching this woman reaching out to grasp her spinning staff, hard at work in her home. Like a good movie director, the writer then switches the action, but her hands are still in the same position. We're transitioned to seeing her use her hands in another context: loving the poor and helping the needy.

The woman in Proverbs 31 didn't think the needy people in her world were someone else's problem to deal with. She didn't ignore them and hope they'd go away, nor was she so focused on herself and the needs of her own family that she overlooked them. She saw them, recognized their needs, and deliberately took action to reach out and meet those needs.

world? This week, Proverbs 31 will issue a challenge to not only care about the poor of the world, but also to actively help others. Will you accept the challenge?

FIRST THINGS FIRST

The best example for how to respond to the poor in this world is Jesus. While you'll dig a little deeper into this topic during Day 1's Bible study, it is important to consider right now. Think about all the stories in the Gospels about the people Jesus healed. A blind man. A bleeding woman. A paralytic. How did He heal them?

Jesus didn't take a hands-off approach and just tell people to "Be healed." Most of the time, when He healed someone, He actually touched the person. He met peoples' physical needs before He even broached the topic of their spiritual needs. While we don't have the ability to heal people simply by touching them, we can help them on the journey of healing their hearts by reaching out our hands and touching them. You might have heard that women need several physical touches a day in order to feel emotionally healthy. A pat on the back or a hug really can change your day.

Imagine if no one ever touched you, or if everyone looked at you with disgust because you smelled bad and couldn't brush your hair or your teeth. Jesus encountered people like that, too, and He didn't turn away. Be more like Him and quit focusing on what the poor look like and how different they are from you, and instead focus on how you can help them.

Jesus went out of His way to help others; so should you. Service is rarely convenient or easy. But even when it is, seek to seize every opportunity that you can to serve.

You'll look a little more like Jesus when you do.

day 1
A deliberate choice

The Proverbs 31 woman's concern for the poor is another one of her important character traits. **Read Proverbs 31:19-20.** Understand this: the capable woman didn't wait to happen upon the poor when she was out walking the sidewalks. She "reached out" to them. That means she was deliberate in helping them.

Answer these questions:

- If she were alive today, in what ways may this woman have reached out to the poor?

- Unlike the woman in Proverbs 31, you're here today. How many of those things are you doing? Explain.

- Do you ever make excuses to avoid helping others in need? What are they? Are they valid? Explain.

While our excuses sound perfectly valid to us, they don't excuse us from what Christ calls us to do. **Look up Matthew 25:31-46 and answer the following questions.**

- What is this passage about?

- What do these verses have to do with how you treat others, particularly those in need?

- How do these verses challenge you to live differently?

While serving the poor can be a great experience and help us feel closer to God, it can also give us a sense of self-righteousness. Have you ever seen someone serve others or do community service just to get the hours for a club or to build their resume? If that's their only purpose for serving, then their motives are wrong. We have to make sure we're serving for the right reasons.

Read Matthew 6:1-4.

- What did Jesus mean when He said "Don't let your left hand know what your right hand is doing"?

- What does that mean for you when you serve the poor or the needy in the future?

If you're still confused on what it should look like when you help the poor and the needy, you have a really good example—Jesus. **Read the following Scripture passages about Jesus and then answer the questions.**

Read Matthew 8:1-4.

- What was wrong with the man?

- What did Jesus do that would have been shocking to the Jews then? (Read Leviticus 13, especially verses 45-46; see also Isaiah 52:11 to understand why touching an "unclean" man was so taboo.)

- What happened to the man?

- How is Jesus' interaction a good example for us?

Read Matthew 9:27-33.

- What was wrong with these two guys?

- What did Jesus ask them?

- How and why did He heal them?

- What was wrong with the other guy who appeared in verse 32?

- What happened after Jesus drove out the demon?

GOING DEEPER:

- What's your attitude toward the needy people in your world? Do you take deliberate action to help them, or do you consider them someone else's problem? Why?

- What specific steps will you take this week to reach out to the poor like the Proverbs 31 woman did? Detail your plan below.

WEEKLY MEMORY VERSE:

"If a brother or sister is without clothes and lacks daily food and one of you says to them, "Go in peace, keep warm, and eat well," but you don't give them what the body needs, what good is it? In the same way faith, if it doesn't have works, is dead by itself."
—James 2:15-17

day 2

Do good

As Christians, we are called to love and glorify God. One of the ways we can show our love for Him is by loving others. And not just the "others" who are like us, but the others who are very different from us. The poor, the desperate, the depressed, the oppressed—these people need our love. And love is shown by actions. Your actions toward the poor show how you feel about them.

Read 1 Timothy 6:18-19, then answer these questions:

- How can you do what is good? What does that even mean?

- Are you rich in good works? Explain.

- In what ways are you generous?

- In what ways are you not generous? How can you be more generous in these areas?

- Do you share well with others? Explain.

- Whom do you typically share your stuff with—your sisters/brothers? Friends? Strangers?

- How do you feel when you share your possessions?

GOING DEEPER:

- You have a lot to be thankful for. List some of those things below.

- Look over that list and put a star beside those things you wouldn't mind sharing. Draw a box around those things that you don't want to share. How do you think Jesus would respond to your unwillingness to share those things that you've drawn a box around? Why? What changes will you make in these areas this week?

- What do your actions toward those in need (be it a family member or a complete stranger) say about your walk with Christ?

- Do you think that your good works please God on a daily basis? Why or why not?

day 3:

Equal footing

Sometimes you may think you're better than others. At other times, you may get pretty down when you compare yourself to people who seem to have everything you want. But the Bible assures us that we're all God's creations. And things (including people!) aren't created without intention. You're here on purpose. And so are the people you compare yourself to, whether they've got it all or if they've got nothing.

Read Job 34:19 and Proverbs 22:2. Answer these questions:

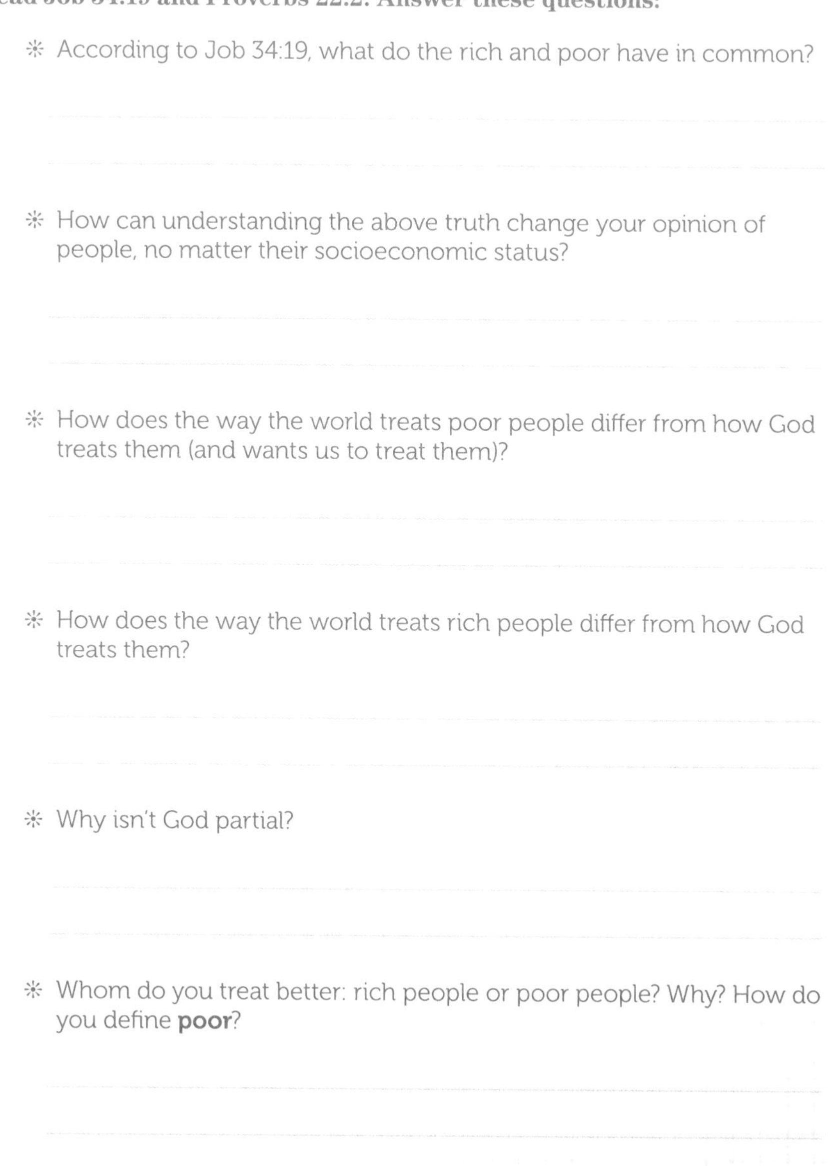

- According to Job 34:19, what do the rich and poor have in common?
- How can understanding the above truth change your opinion of people, no matter their socioeconomic status?
- How does the way the world treats poor people differ from how God treats them (and wants us to treat them)?
- How does the way the world treats rich people differ from how God treats them?
- Why isn't God partial?
- Whom do you treat better: rich people or poor people? Why? How do you define **poor**?

GOING DEEPER:

- Think of people you treat differently because of what they do or do not have. How can you love them equally? List some practical ideas.

- When you encounter the poor, how should you view them now that we've studied this topic? How will that change the way you treat them? If you consider yourself to be poor, how has this study challenged your thoughts about your family's situation? Explain.

- Think of some of your favorite smells. Cookies baking, your favorite perfume, the smell of clothes straight out of the dryer. List them below.

- Now think about some of the smells you might encounter as you serve the poor. (Dirty living conditions, bad breath, body odor, etc.) List them if you like. How will you overcome these barriers to help people who truly need it?

- Identify a few people you know of in your community who are in need. What can you do to reach out to them? Write out a plan of action to serve the poor or those who need your help this week.

day 4

All the right reasons

Loving those who need our help results in two benefits for us: We fulfill God's command to "Love your neighbor as yourself" (Mark 12:31), and we are blessed in ways we could never have imagined. Whether it's the satisfaction of knowing we did the right thing, the "thank you" from the person we helped, or just the knowledge that God saw our act and was pleased, doing good, especially for the poor, pleases God and blesses us—so much so that Scripture says God will save the one who cares for the poor on a day of adversity.

Read Psalm 41:1 and Mark 12:31, then answer these questions:

- Have you ever experienced joy after caring for the poor (or weak)?
- If so, why do you think you felt that way?
- What was your attitude about helping the poor/weak before you helped?
- Did it change after you served? If so, how?
- Have you ever experienced God rescuing you in a time of trouble or adversity? Explain.

- What does it mean to love others as you love yourself? Why is that important to God?

- What are some practical steps you can take to love others that way today?

GOING DEEPER:

- How does loving others show your love for God? What does it tell the world?

- If you were an outsider looking at your life, would your life say anything about God's love to the world? Why or why not? What changes will you make this week so that it does demonstrate His love more?

day 5

Give and receive

You might have heard it said that your actions come back to you. While you've probably heard sayings like that attributed to a Hindu belief called karma, the Bible actually has something to say about what you can expect from your actions: whether they're good or bad, you reap what you sow (Hosea 8:7).

How we treat others is no exception. God rewards us for the good we do, and He also takes note of the opportunities to do good that we avoid.

Read Proverbs 14:21; 28:27; and James 4:17, then answer these questions:

- How is Proverbs 14:21 similar to Psalm 41:1 (from yesterday)?

- How is it different?

- What good things are promised to the person who gives to someone in need?

- Have you ever turned your eyes away from or closed them to someone in need? If so, how did it make you feel? If you could go back to that situation, what would you do differently?

- What does James 4:17 say about those opportunities to do good that we have but don't take?

- How does that change your opinion of those opportunities?

GOING DEEPER:

Put yourself in someone else's shoes for a second. Imagine you're homeless. No house. No warm bed. No kitchen to cook in. No bathroom to bathe in. Think of how different your life would be. Then ask yourself these questions:

- If you were homeless, how would you want to be treated?
- What would be important to you?
- What would be the best way for someone to minister to you?

Develop a plan of action for what you'll do the next time you see someone in need. Think about the following circumstances, then come up with some of your own:

- If you see a homeless person, what will you do? **(Can you put any of your ideas from the previous questions into practice?)**
- If you see someone at school who is alone or upset, how will you respond?

- If you hear about a ministry that is working to share God's love and meet people's needs, but is struggling (financially, with not having enough volunteers or supplies, etc.), what will you do to help?

day 6

Is your faith alive?

We've spent a lot of time this week looking at loving others, especially the poor. We love others by serving them, meeting their needs, and showing them (with our words and actions) that they are valued. Reading and thinking about service are one thing. Actually getting out of your comfort zone and embracing the needy is another.

But it speaks volumes about your faith. If you're not meeting needs when you see them, it doesn't speak well of your relationship with God. After all, He was willing to give it all for you. Why aren't you willing to do the same for others?

No really, think about it. Why aren't you?

Read James 2:14-24. Answer these questions:

- In verses 15-16, the writer of James said that wishing someone well is not the same as meeting their needs. When have you seen a similar scenario in today's world?

- Why do you think the writer says faith without works is useless?

- Is the writer saying that salvation is dependent on our works? Explain.

* What has God called you to sacrifice?

* Is there anything in your life that will be credited to you as righteousness? Explain.

GOING DEEPER:

The writer of James was not saying that we must have works to get into heaven. Jesus did all the work necessary to save us from our sins. What the writer *is* saying is that a faith without actions makes one wonder if the faith was there to begin with. If you've truly encountered Christ, then your heart should break for those who can't meet their own needs. You should want to serve. So ask yourself:

* Have you ever had your heart break for others? What was the situation?

* How did you help? How do you wish you could have helped?

⁜ If you haven't hurt for others, why do you think that is?

⁜ What motivation do you have to serve others?

day 7

A day for reflection

Read the following Scriptures and write about each below, explaining to God how these verses changed the way you treat others:

- Proverbs 11:25

- Proverbs 19:17

- Proverbs 22:9

- Matthew 5:42

> She is not afraid for her household when it snows, for all in her household are doubly clothed. Strength and honor are her clothing, and she can laugh at the time to come.
>
> —Proverbs 31:21,25

week 6

not anxious about the future

INTRODUCTION TO WEEK 6

How much time do you spend thinking about the future? Maybe you spend a lot of time fretting about where to go to college, what to major in, whom you'll marry, how many kids you'll have, and where you'll live. Or maybe you can't seem to get past that big test you've got next week or who will ask you to the dance at the end of the month. No matter how far into the future you let your mind wander, don't get too far ahead of yourself. Today is your main priority.

As females, it's easy to live in a dream world of future possibilities. Dreams aren't bad things to have and hold onto, especially when they're God-given. But while the future is yet to come, you've got to get through today to get there. Yet you worry about what the future will bring.

No matter what the future holds for you, the key to handling it well is being prepared. If you want to know God better when you're older, dig into His Word today. If you know you have a test coming up, use today to study for it. If you know you want to get into a certain college some day, start researching today about the requirements for admission. If you dream of getting married, start the process today of becoming a woman who will make a godly wife.

THIS WEEK'S THEME

In the past few weeks you've learned a lot about the Proverbs 31 woman. She's wise, trustworthy, diligent, a hard worker, smart, strong, and cares about others. This week your study will focus on Proverbs 31:21,25, which reveal that our capable woman is not anxious about the future.

Proverbs 31 isn't the only place Scripture deals with the problem of worrying. In the Sermon on the Mount, Jesus said:

> "Don't worry about your life, what you will eat or what you will drink; or about your body, what you will wear. Isn't life more than food and the body more than clothing?" —Matthew 6:25

Back in college, I started writing down what was worrying me in the margins around this passage in my Bible. Things like acne, finding a job after college, and finding a place to live once I found a job are all written in various shades of ink with various dates. And you know what, God took care of every single one of my concerns! A smile always crosses my face when I happen upon that page and see all of those former worries.

And that's not all Scripture has to say on the topic. In Matthew 6:34 we're instructed not to worry about tomorrow because it has enough troubles of its own. In Philippians 4:6, we're told not to worry about anything, but "but in everything, through prayer and petition with thanksgiving" make our requests known to God Himself.

As believers, our lives are supposed to be controlled by the Holy Spirit, not by relentless fear or worry. But in a world we can't control, it's easy to let worry creep into your life and steal the joy we've been given as followers of Christ. *What if she's diagnosed with cancer? What if I fail this test? What if he doesn't like me? What if I bare my soul to him and he just walks away? What if I'm not good enough, pretty enough, smart enough, or simply just not enough?*

Stop! Read God's promise in Hebrews 13:5b. What does it say?

"I will never leave you or forsake you." —Hebrews 13:5b

God will never leave you, and if something matters to you, it matters to God. He's with you in your worries and longs to lift the burden of carrying them off your shoulders. Remember Jesus' words in Matthew 11:29-30:

"All of you, take up My yoke and learn from Me, because I am gentle and humble in heart, and you will find rest for yourselves. For My yoke is easy and My burden is light." —Matthew 11:29-30

Cast your burdens, worries included, upon the Lord. Do not be anxious about anything. Instead, lift your worries and fears to God. He will never leave you or forsake you.

day 1

Not afraid of the future

In your study of the Proverbs 31 woman, you've learned a lot about her work ethic, trustworthiness, and business sense. Today you'll see how she handled things beyond her control, including the future. **Please read Proverbs 31:21,25.**

- Why isn't the Proverbs 31 woman afraid when cold weather hits?

- What does it mean to be "doubly" clothed?

- How does the woman's preparation help her not to worry?

There is some disagreement over the exact meaning of the word "doubly," as it can also mean "scarlet," which would have meant that the clothing was of a superior quality. Whether they were dressed in layers or in the highest-quality garments, the Proverb 31 woman's family was well-clothed and didn't have to worry about the weather.

✳ Have you ever not been dressed right for the weather? In the space below, tell (or draw) what you had on and what the weather was like.

Verse 25 reveals the true character of this woman. "Strength and honor are her clothing, and she can laugh at the time to come." In addition to the physical clothes she puts on each morning, this woman also clothed herself in strength and honor.

We're commanded in Scripture to clothe ourselves with several things. Please read the following verses and write out what we are to put on, as believers.

1 Peter 5:5: __________

Ephesians 6:11-17: __________

Romans 13:11-14: __________

Ephesians 4:22-24: __________

Colossians 3:9-15: __________

In additional to her physical strength, it's becoming clear that the Proverbs 31 woman possesses a different type of strength, one that the *New Oxford American Dictionary*[1] defines as "the emotional or mental qualities necessary in dealing with situations or events that are distressing or difficult." She's capable of feeding lots of people, working long hours, selling her own goods to merchants, and putting in physical labor in her vineyard and at her spinning wheel. She also works to meet the needs of the poor. None of these are easy, and yet she meets each challenge.

One of the things I like most about her is found at the end of verse 25: "She can laugh at the time to come." As a recovering worrier, this verse is refreshing. This woman worked hard each day to prepare for whatever the future might bring. Her kitchen was stocked, her family was clothed, and she had her own stream of income. If something crazy happened, then she could probably handle it (and laugh at it). But even if it was beyond her control, she knows who's got it under control—her God.

You can do the same. You can glance at the future and make sure your actions today will not have a negative effect on it. You can work hard today at activities that will have a positive effect on your future (like studying, perfecting your pitch in softball or choir, practicing the routine some more, and eating well). But if you forget who's actually got the future under control, you may cross the line into obsessing about it. If you're letting your worry over the future affect today, Jesus has something to say to you in Matthew 6:25-34.

Read Matthew 6:25-34. Remember how I said I write things that worry me in my Bible near this passage? Think about a few things that are worrying you right now. Big deals, small issues, whatever. **If it worries you, write it down, along with the date.** Then, every few months, review this list. See how God has taken care of the things that worry you. If you'd rather write some worries here, do so in the space provided.

As I said before, I used to worry a lot. I worried about my dad losing his job. I worried about being abandoned at school every time my ride was late. I worried about tests and papers. But I worried most about being in a bad car wreck and being badly injured or dying. It happened to so many people, and I just knew it was going to happen to me. But I came to the realization that God was in control, and I wasn't. I began to understand that if I was involved in a car wreck, then God had allowed it to happen. It hadn't happened apart from His knowledge; in fact, He had approved it for my life. And if it was part of His plan for my life, then I was going to accept it and know that I would have Him to lean on to get through it. Let's try to be like the Proverbs 31 woman by preparing for the future as best we can, then letting God handle the rest. I promise you'll laugh a lot more if you do!

GOING DEEPER:

- Having a bad wreck is just my example. Is there something you're worrying about that you may not have even written down because it just seems so out there? Tell God about that worry, too. (He already knows it.) Write it, draw it, or even record your prayer about it here.

* Do you let worry about what might happen rob you of your joy in following Christ? In addition to praying about your worries, talk to your mom or a trusted Christian woman about your anxiety. Work together to create a list of practical steps you can take when worry overwhelms you. Write them here.

WEEKLY MEMORY VERSE:

"Don't worry about anything, but in everything, through prayer and petition with thanksgiving, let your requests be made known to God."
—Philippians 4:6

[1] "Strength," New Oxford American Dictionary, 2007 [electronic resource].

day 2

Do not worry

You may not worry so much about meeting your basic needs, like having food, clothing, and shelter. But you may worry about your appearance and things the world says are important. Worry is tricky because it paralyzes us with the "what if" when the "what if" may not even happen. God knows what we need, and He knows what is going to happen to us. Do you trust Him?

For a slightly different look at a Scripture you've already studied, read Luke 12:22-34. Answer these questions:

* What does Jesus command in verse 22? How well do you follow that command? Explain.

* What should you be seeking instead of worrying about what you think you need?

* What is the radical teaching in verses 33 and 34? What does that look like in your life?

* Honestly evaluate the treasures of your heart. Are you storing up treasures in heaven or here on earth? Explain.

* What does it mean to be a part of Jesus' "little flock"? (See v. 32.) How does this endearment show His love and tenderness toward us?

* How does worry interfere with your relationship with Christ?

GOING DEEPER:

- ✻ What things are you worrying about that you have absolutely no control over? Why do you worry about them? How can you turn them over to God? List and pray about these situations right now. Write your prayer below.

- ✻ What things are you worrying about that you can control? Have you actually spent time preparing for those things, or are you allowing the worry to occupy your time? Explain. Write a list of ways you can prepare for these things.

- ✻ How does worry affect you physically? Mentally? Emotionally? How is it affecting your relationship with God right now? What steps will you take today to give your worries over to Him?

day 3:

Despite the circumstances

Have you ever seen a friend allow circumstances to get the best of him or her? He lashes out in anger at friends who weren't being serious with their teasing remarks. She freaks out because the teacher accidentally lost her paper. He hauls off and hits some guy because he thought the guy was flirting with his girlfriend. As Christians, we aren't called to be emotionless—but we are called to realize that our response to situations in life should be shaped by and reflect who we are in Christ.

Read Jeremiah 17:7-8 and Psalm 1:2-3. Answer these questions:

- Jeremiah 17:8 contains a simile. In this simile, who is the tree? Who is the water?
- Why doesn't a tree planted by a stream have to worry about heat and drought?
- During difficult seasons of life, why don't Christians need to worry? Explain.
- If you're in the middle of a season of worry, have you stopped producing fruit? Why or why not?
- What caused delight in Psalm 1:2?

- Do you think that if you concentrated on something day and night that it would bring you delight? Why or why not?

- Do you take delight in the Lord's instruction (the Bible)? Why or why not?

- Jeremiah 17:7-8 and Psalm 1:2-3 both refer to a tree planted beside a water source. How do these verses reveal you can become like these trees, unafraid of what the future brings?

GOING DEEPER:

- In what areas of your life do you not trust God? List them here. Spend some time praying over these areas.

- How can you trust God more in these areas ? What are some practical ways to do so?

* Part of overcoming worry is recognizing God is faithful and trustworthy. One way to learn that is to spend time reading Scripture. What can you do to spend more time with God and in His Word? Write your action plan below.

day 4:

How to get rid of worry

How do you deal with worry? Do you try to take care of it yourself by staying busy and preparing for every possible outcome? The Bible's approach to handling worry is a lot easier than that. Paul instructs us to take everything that worries us to God in prayer.

Read Philippians 4:6-7. Answer these questions:

* What do these verses have to do with eliminating worry?

* When you present a request to God, do you express gratitude to God for hearing and answering?

* How often do you take your requests to God?

* Would you say you are persistent in your prayers? Why or why not?

※ What does verse 7 say will happen after you take your request to God?

※ Is that comforting to you? Why or why not?

※ What does it mean that God's peace will guard your heart and your mind when you give Him everything in prayer? How have you seen that play out in real life?

GOING DEEPER:

※ Around the word **peace** below, write all the words related to peace that come to mind.

peace

※ Have you ever experienced the peace of God? If so, describe that time. If not, describe what you think it would be like.

- If you have experienced the peace of God, would you say that it "surpasses every thought" or "transcends all understanding" (Phil. 4:6-7, depending on your translation)? Why or why not? If not, had you truly surrendered your worry to the Lord?

day 5

He's got your future

You have a huge role to play in shaping your future. Your decisions (both good and bad) will affect who you become and how God can use you. But that's not to say that you are ultimately responsible for everything your life is supposed to accomplish. God created you for a reason, and He will bring His plan for you to completion. You have a purpose!

Are the things on your mind today going to help you or hinder you in fulfilling that purpose? (Knowing God and glorifying Him are **always** your purpose.)

Read Psalm 16:5-11. Answer these questions:

- The psalmist said God was his portion, all he needed. Is that true about your relationship with God? Is He all you need? Explain.

- Do you look to other things (like boys, money, looks, grades, and so forth) to fulfill you? Why or why not?

- Why is it important to recognize that God—not you—holds your future? Do you live like you believe that truth? Why or why not? What needs to change?

- Do you believe that the plan God has for you is "pleasant" or "beautiful"? Why or why not?

- Pick out a few of the verses that stood out to you in the Scripture passage you read and rewrite them below, in your own words.

GOING DEEPER:

- Be honest. What about leaving your future in God's hands scares you? Why?

- ⁜ What would living out verse 8 look like in your life tomorrow? Be practical!

day 6: Why you can trust Him

You've probably read the verse we're going to look at today before. It's quoted at high school graduations, written in yearbooks, and loved by many people—some of whom love it because they long for life to be easy. But there's a following verse that often gets overlooked. And it might make you realize that you have to put forth some effort before you can embrace those plans the Lord has for you.

Read Jeremiah 29:11-13. Answer these questions:

- ⁜ Verse 11 says God knows the plans He has for us, but verse 12 offers some advice on how we seek and discover those plans. What is that advice? How does it challenge you?

- ⁜ Are you using your whole heart to find Him? Why or why not? Be honest—just you and God are going to see this.

- ⁜ How often do you call to God, go to Him, and pray to Him, like in verse 12? Explain. How does seeking God help you to know His plan for your life?

⁂ Do you believe that God listens to you? Why or why not?

⁂ Because you know God's plans are to give you a future and a hope, what comfort do you find in that? Why?

GOING DEEPER:

Set aside some time today to pray, like verse 12 instructs. Know that God will hear you. What would you like to tell Him about your future, about worry, about anything? Be sure to spend some time listening, too, because prayer isn't all about you talking. It's also about listening for God's still, small voice.

Read aloud some of the Scriptures we've covered this week. Use them as a conversation starter between you and God by substituting yourself into the Scripture. (Verses 12 and 13 of today's reading become: "I will call to You and come and pray to You, God, and You will listen to me. I will seek You and find You when I search for You with all my heart.")

Feel free to use the space below for reflections or how you think God would respond to you.

day 7

A day for reflection

Read the following Scriptures and write a sentence or two about each verse below, explaining to God how these verses challenged, changed, and encouraged you:

- Psalm 16

- Psalm 56:3-13

- Hebrews 13:5-6

Her husband is known at the city gates, where he sits among the elders of the land.

—Proverbs 31:23

week 7
the right kind of guy

INTRODUCTION TO WEEK 7

Do you think about being married one day? It's normal to wonder if you'll get married, identify some characteristics you want your future husband to have and think about your future with him. List a few ideas of the kind of guy you're looking for here:

First and foremost, if you are a believer, then you are not supposed to be dating a non-Christian (2 Cor. 6:14-15). So if the guy you like isn't a believer, then you need to break up with him or quit crushing on him. (It's hard, but it really is for the best.)

OK, so now that we've settled that, consider this: Even if your boyfriend or the guy you like isn't popular or making straight A's, it's important that he exhibit the following qualities, as they show that he is seeking God's will and will earn respect from others in his life:

- **Intelligence:** Does he use the mind God gave him, or does he depend on others to tell him how to answer questions and solve problems (both in and outside of the classroom)?
- **Integrity:** Does he do the right thing at all times and at all costs?
- **Discipline:** Is he attempting to learn? Does he try to improve? Does he apply himself (to school, sports, music)?
- **Diligence:** Is he consistent? Does he follow through on things he says he'll do?
- **Wisdom:** Does he usually have sound advice to offer? Does he make good choices?
- **Determination:** Does he have the will to persevere when things aren't easy?
- **Godliness:** Most importantly, is he seeking God daily?

A guy with these qualities uses his God-given abilities to make wise choices that usually benefit others. And because of this, he will be respected by other men. They may not like him or what he has to say, but they will more than likely esteem him, speak well of him to others, and listen to him when he speaks.

Now, this is not saying that you should aspire to marry someone well-known or wealthy. Often, the well-known and the wealthy in our society don't have these qualities. Think about the celebrity crushes you've had, then answer these questions:

❊ What types of relationships are those guys in now?

- Why are those guys well-known? (Most of those things are not what should make a person famous anyway.)

- Do they possess the important qualities we talked about earlier (i.e. intelligence, integrity, discipline, diligence, wisdom, determination, godliness)?

As a Proverbs 31 girl, the guys you date should meet some pretty important standards!

THIS WEEK'S THEME:

Remember how we talked about chiastic structure the first week? (See page 7.) Well, we're at the middle of it, the hinge. Verse 23 is directed at the poem's audience, young men. Please read this verse in your Bible.

Proverbs personifies wisdom as a woman. Proverbs 3:13-18 repeatedly tells its audience (which, when the proverbs were written, were young men) to get wisdom. Wisdom is then embodied in the woman you're studying. Her qualities allowed her husband to flourish. If you get married, you can either exalt or destroy your husband with your actions. If you get married, it will be your God-given role to create an environment in which your husband can flourish. (And he should be doing the same for you!) When a man is encouraged and cared for by his wife, he'll be better able to do the things that will earn him respect from others.

The verse you read today is a charge to the man that he aspire to be esteemed even by his elders and earn a position of respect in the city. Having a wife like the one in Proverbs 31 would earn the respect of others as well. Her trustworthiness, work ethic, business sense, and ability to bring good things to him and his household make it clear that she's quite a catch, and he must be a decent man himself in order to be loved by her. Clearly, this guy is intelligent and wise because we see that he's well known in the city and respected by city officials.

I realize that you're still in school. Chances are that the guys you're around are still immature at times, are not in positions of power in your town, and are just trying to get through school with passing grades—not find a wife of noble character! But that doesn't mean that those guys aren't on your mind.

Spill! Record below whom you have a crush on and why.

Now it's time to see if he lives up the standards of a godly girl like you!

day 1

The right guy

It's pretty clear that a Proverbs 31 kind of girl doesn't date (or marry) any guy. Instead, she's knows the importance of finding a quality guy who loves Jesus and lives accordingly. But what does that mean for you, right now?

Read Proverbs 31:23. Answer the following questions.

- What does this verse tell you about the Proverbs 31 woman's husband?

- Does this verse shed any light on the kind of qualities you should look for in the guy you date?

- Remember that Proverbs 31 was written as instructions to young men. If you were the author of the Book of Proverbs and were writing Proverbs 31 to young women, what would you say? Mirroring the current verses, outline for a young woman the type of man who qualifies as a "Capable Husband."

QUIZ:

Let's look at the guy whom you're currently dating or wanting to date. Think of him as you take the following quiz. Circle your answers:

- Does he treat you well when you're with others? Yes No

- Does he treat you well when you're alone? Yes No

- Does he talk openly with you about what he's thinking? Yes No

- Does he talk openly with his parents about his relationship with you? Yes No

- ✻ Do your parents like him? Yes No
- ✻ Does he talk about the future a lot ("When we get married," "when we have kids . . .")? Yes No
- ✻ Does he pressure you to go further than you'd like to physically? (Even just a little further?) Yes No
- ✻ Does he ever make you feel stupid? Yes No
- ✻ Does he pay attention to what you say? Yes No
- ✻ Do you feel like he understands you better than anyone else? Yes No
- ✻ Does he teach you how to do new things? Yes No
- ✻ Does he encourage you? Yes No
- ✻ Do you two read and discuss Scripture together? Yes No
- ✻ Do you pray for each other? Yes No
- ✻ Do you think God approves of your relationship? Yes No

GOING DEEPER:

- ✻ If you answered no to that last question, I want you to take steps this week to remedy the situation or end the relationship/infatuation with the guy. Why waste your time with the wrong guy? Write the steps you'll take this week.

High school relationships have a lot of promise. But they also may cause you a lot of heartache. Your hormones are running amok, and I know you want to act on them. And guys want you to act on them. But if you've been in church for awhile, you know that it's God's plan for you to wait until you are married to have sex. Once you get started (even with heavy, prolonged kissing), it's hard to stop. And all those pre-sex acts you may think are OK (like oral sex, touching each other, and whatever else you're doing when you're alone in the dark) are not OK. It's just making you want more of what you can't have. When you build a bond of physical intimacy with someone (even if you haven't technically had sex with him), it is going to make it harder and harder for you to end the relationship with him. It could drag out for years as jealousy and attachment prevent you from getting out of a relationship that clearly isn't healthy.

- What behaviors do you need to stop this week? Write a plan for how you'll do so.

- Have you made a commitment to remain sexually pure until marriage? If not, why not do that now? Write your commitment below, then sign and date it. Tell your parents about it and consider making it public with a True Love Waits commitment ceremony at your church. Find out more about TLW at **www.truelovewaits.com**.

- If you're not in a relationship, don't lament that. Read 1 Corinthians 7:34. Use the time that God has given you by yourself to get to know Him—and yourself! Take time to read the Bible, especially Scripture about what a godly man looks like, so you'll know what you're looking for in any guy you'll date in the future. Learn about how a godly woman acts; work on becoming one. How will you spend your time becoming the woman God wants you to be this week? Record your ideas below.

WEEKLY MEMORY VERSE:

"But you, man of God, run from these things, and pursue righteousness, godliness, faith, love, endurance, and gentleness."
—1 Timothy 6:11

- Dating in high school can be fun, but you shouldn't take it too lightly. You're learning about guys. They're learning about girls. Train yourself to evaluate every guy against the standard God set in Ephesians 5:22-31. How does this Scripture affect whom you will date? Write a list of qualities the guy you marry (and date!) needs to embody.

day 2:

What a godly man should be

What kind of man do you hope to marry? During this study, we've talked about the qualities a man should have. But maybe you're thinking to yourself, "Hey, I'm not looking to get married right now; I'm in high school! I just want to be in a fun relationship. I want someone to talk to, to hang out with, to go places with. What's wrong with that?"

Well, nothing. But we just want to make sure you're still taking very seriously whom you spend your time with and making sure that if you and your parents have decided you're ready to date, that you're being selective.

Read 1 Timothy 6:9-12. Answer these questions:

- What characteristics should a man of God possess?

- What should he pursue? Why?

- What is the warning in verses 9 and 10? Why is that important?

* Do you know people who have ignored that warning? If so, what do their lives look like?

* How is the love of money is a root of all kinds of evil?

* How can you help the guys in your life pursue the qualities outlined in this passage? Be practical!

GOING DEEPER:

* Is there a guy in your life who needs your encouragement to be a man of God? Perhaps he likes you and won't leave you alone, but you don't like him. Maybe it's a guy you're dating who needs some encouragement to grow in his relationship with God. Maybe it's your dad or brother. What specific actions will you take today to help the guys around you be godly men?

* Reread today's Scripture passage, 1 Timothy 6:9-12. What warnings and lessons can a girl like you take away from this passage? Write them below.

day 3:

What a godly man studies

You're busy. You've got so much on your plate between school, sports, work, and church, that you probably don't have a lot of time to read the Bible. But maybe you know some people who do make time to study it.

What do you think about the guys at school or in youth group who actually know what the Bible says? Do you think they're weird? Or do you respect them? Would you say that the guys you know are as knowledgeable about the Bible as you are? Why or why not?

Read 2 Timothy 3:16-17. Answer these questions:

- According to this passage, what is Scripture good for?

- Have you ever seen Scripture used in any of the ways listed in verse 16? If so, explain.

- When was the last time that Scripture made a difference in your life? Write about it here.

- How can studying the Bible help a guy know what to do?

- Why is it important that you date guys who study the Bible?

GOING DEEPER:

- Did you know that the Bible applies to your life today? If you answered yes, how did you come to that knowledge? If you answered no, why do you think the Bible doesn't apply to your life today?

- How will you study the Word of God this week in order to know it well enough to apply it to situations in your life? (Consider memorizing Scripture, committing to reading the whole Bible in a year, or taking some other approach to know the Word.) Write down your commitment below, then sign and date it.

I, ____________________ *(your full name)*, promise to __________

in order to learn more about the Holy Word of God so that I can apply it to my life.

Signature

Date

day 4

How a godly man prays

Prayer is important for believers. It is our direct line of communication with God. While God always hears our prayers, He doesn't just answer our wish list or do whatever we ask. God isn't Santa Claus. The fact is, when you're living with integrity and seeking God, your prayers reflect that and begin to line up with His will. Because your prayers are already in tune with the desires of God, He will answer them, though maybe not on your timetable.

Read John 9:30-33 and James 5:13-16. Answer these questions:

- What does John 9:31 say is necessary for God to hear what you pray about?

- Skim John 9 in its entirety. What happened in John 9 that gave evidence that Jesus was from God?

- Do you know anyone who is "God-fearing"? If so, what about his or her life sets him or her apart?

- What does doing God's will have to do with Him answering your prayers?

- How is the prayer of a righteous person is powerful and effective, as it says in James 5:15? When have you seen this in real life?

- Why is it important that the guys you date (and ultimately, the man you'll marry) be righteous?

GOING DEEPER:

Spend several moments praying for your future husband. Ask God to help him grow in his relationship with God now and to live a life that you'll be proud to be a part of one day. Pray also that God will allow you to learn more about Him and His Word as He shapes you into a godly woman. Write out your prayer below.

day 5:

A godly man walks in integrity

Life isn't easy—but how you respond to troubles in life makes a difference. How do the men or guys in your life handle problems? Do they get angry, frustrated, or upset? Or do they respond calmly and carefully, with wisdom? How do you think the guy you're currently interested in or most recently dated would handle tough situations (losing a job, death of a loved one, argument with a friend)?

Read Proverbs 20:7; Job 1:1,8-22; 2:7-10; 28:12-28; 42:10-17.

- Focus on Proverbs 20:7. What benefit is there for a man of integrity?

- Reflect on your own family. Do you see the promise of Proverbs 20:7 lived out in your family? Explain.

- Reread the verses from Job. Why did God have confidence in Job? Do you think God has the same kind of confidence in you? Why or why not?

- When Job questioned God, how did God respond?

- Will the passages you studied today have an impact on how you look at the guys you know and might consider dating? How so?

GOING DEEPER:

- Put yourself in Job's position. Imagine the tragedy he endured. Write about how you would have responded to all he had to face. How would you have been like Job? How would you have responded differently?

- Now, pretend your dad (or some other man who is important to you) is in Job's shoes. How would he react to all that tragedy?

- Is integrity in the guys you date important to you? Think about the guys you've dated, the one you are dating, or the guys you're kind of interested in. Is integrity a big deal to them? How do you know?

day 6

A godly man is disciplined

An athlete in training. A recovering alcoholic. A soldier. What do they have in common? They will fail without discipline. Similarly, a man (or woman) cannot be haphazard in his (or her) approach to a relationship with God. We are saved by grace, but in order to grow in that relationship, there are some very specific things we have to do and a standard we should desire to live by.

One of those is our sexuality. Let's face it: Romance takes up a lot of your thoughts. For guys, sex takes up a lot of theirs. Sex and romance are two sides of the same coin. While it's a desire you may want to satisfy, the Bible has plenty to say about those desires.

Read 1 Corinthians 9:25; 6:18-20, then answer these questions.

- In 1 Corinthians 9:25, how is the training described?

- Why do you think it's described that way?

- What does self-control have to do with our discussion of sex and romance?

- Is the "crown" worth the effort to you? Why or why not?

- In 1 Corinthians 6:18-20, why are you told to honor God with your body? What does it mean to honor God with your body? List a few specific ideas about how to do so?

⁂ In what ways have you not honored God with your body in the past?

⁂ What was the price at which you were bought (v. 20)? How does knowing you were bought with a price change or challenge the way you're living?

⁂ What are some other areas of your life in which discipline is needed?

GOING DEEPER:

⁂ Guys cannot fight the battle for sexual purity on their own. How can you help the guys around you keep their thoughts pure? List your ideas.

- Setting boundaries is important, but you won't uphold them without accountability. Whom can you ask to help you protect your purity? How will they keep you accountable?

- How will you respond to a guy you want to date/are dating who has different views from yours on purity?

day 7

A day for reflection

Read the following Scriptures and write about each below, explaining to God how these verses had an impact on you:

- Ephesians 5:25,28-33

- 1 Corinthians 7:25-35

- 1 Peter 3:1-7

She opens her mouth with wisdom and loving instruction is on her tongue.

—Proverbs 31:26

week 8
wise words

INTRODUCTION TO WEEK 8

Women tend to use words to wound others. It's a fact. Ever been the victim of gossip? Ever been called a name that left you crying in the bathroom? Words can hurt, can't they?

What about the words you use? Whom have you hurt with your words? Maybe it was your mom when you insulted her cooking. Or your younger sibling, when you called him or her fat, annoying, stupid, or anything else that seemed appropriate at the time. Maybe you've hurt your best friend or boyfriend by not thinking before you spoke.

But words can also be used to heal, to lift up, and to love. How many compliments given to you do you still remember? Do you have any words of encouragement from someone important that you like to recall and repeat to yourself when you're feeling discouraged? When have you seen your positive words completely turn a situation around?

Our words are so powerful. They can be used for good or for evil. Proverbs 18:21 is pretty clear on that topic. Look it up. What does it say?

"Life and death are in the power of the tongue, and those who love it will eat its fruit." —Proverbs 18:21

That's right. We have a chance to speak life or death every time we open our mouths to talk. We can choose our words wisely, speaking life into the people around us, or we can use them as weapons, wounding everyone we meet.

Scripture actually has a lot to say on the topic of what we say. Just look up James 3:5-8. Here, we see that the tongue is "set on fire by hell." That kind of explains where some of those hateful things you say come from, doesn't it? Sometimes you didn't even truly mean the awful thing you just said. When you thought about it afterwards, you knew that you should have said something different or not said anything at all. Unfortunately, the damage was already done.

Read James 1:26 to see what it says about not controlling your tongue.

"If anyone thinks he is religious without controlling his tongue, then his religion is useless and he deceives himself." —James 1:26

If you don't control your tongue, your religion is worthless?! Ouch! But sadly, it's true. Every time you speak without thinking and utter unwise words in an attempt to tear down others, build yourself up, or win an argument, you discredit yourself and the God you claim to serve.

But maybe the things you say aren't necessarily mean and hateful. Perhaps it's the way you say them that gets you in trouble. Proverbs 21:23 says, "The one who guards his mouth and tongue keeps himself out of trouble." So if we guard our mouths, we won't get into trouble? Sounds like a plan, but how do we guard our mouths? By guarding our hearts.

THIS WEEK'S THEME

If you haven't caught on yet, this week's study of Proverbs 31 will center on **the power of your words.** Go ahead and read Proverbs 31:26 and start taking notice of how and when the Proverbs 31 woman talks. Does anything in this verse describe you?

The fact is, it's easy to let our mouths run away from us. The Proverbs 31 woman speaks with wisdom and love, which leads me to believe her words are full of life rather than death, as Proverbs 18:21 put it. **Read Matthew 12:34 and Luke 6:45**. What kind of evil things come out of your mouth and your friends' mouths?

If the things coming out of your mouth aren't building good relationships with the people you're speaking to, then maybe you need to examine your heart. If you're listening to music or watching movies full of swearing, then don't be surprised when those words start showing up in your everyday conversations. If you're around people who are constantly screaming at you (and others) or getting all dramatic, don't be surprised if you start behaving that way, too.

But on the flip side, if you're around people who are encouraging and loving, you'll find yourself reaching out in the same way. And if you listen to music, watch movies, and read books that are uplifting and aren't full of cussing, screaming, or girl drama, then you just might find that your mind-set and the things coming out of your mouth are good.

The good news is that God knows what you're about to say. (Well, that's also bad news sometimes, right?) Read Psalm 139:4. If He knows what you're going to say, then surely He can help you not say it. Philippians 4:13 says you can do all things through Christ who strengthens you. If you're wanting the things that come out of your mouth to build up others, endear them to you, and demonstrate the wisdom that God has given you, then He can help you.

But you have to want to make that change. And this week's study of Proverbs 31:26 might help you do so!

day 1

A wise woman speaks wise words

Tired of the drama, misunderstandings, and problems words can cause? Let's look at how the Proverbs 31 woman uses her words. *(Hint: she isn't just saying whatever she wants with no regard for others!)*

Read Proverbs 31:26 in your Bible. Then answer the following questions.

❊ What does it mean that the Proverbs 31 woman opened her mouth with wisdom?

❊ Do you open your mouth with wisdom? Why or why not?

❊ What is loving instruction? Do you give instruction lovingly? Explain.

❊ If the Proverbs 31 woman speaks loving instruction, what does that say about the way she speaks to others?

The Proverbs 31 woman spoke with wisdom, meaning she spoke with knowledge, experience, and good judgment. The things that came out of her mouth were worth listening to, but I'd like to also venture a guess that the way in which she said those things made someone want to listen to them. How many times have you opened your mouth and said something without really thinking it through? Write about it below.

WEEKLY MEMORY VERSE:

"If anyone thinks he is religious without controlling his tongue, then his religion is useless and he deceives himself."
—James 1:26

Your words were mean, misunderstood, or embarrassing to you, right? Have you ever wished you could take back your words?

The woman in Proverbs 31 thought carefully about not only what she would say, but also when and how she would say it. We know she not only spoke with wisdom, but that loving instruction was on her tongue. We've all received instruction from teachers, mothers, fathers, and authority figures.

* How much of that instruction was loving? What do you remember most: the loving times of instruction or the harsh ones? Why?

* In what tone of voice do you picture "loving instruction" being given?

* Do you know of a teacher or parent who is the epitome of giving "loving instruction"? When they tell you to do something with loving instruction, how do you respond? How do you feel? Why is loving instruction so powerful?

Here's the deal: just because instruction is loving doesn't mean it doesn't hurt the feelings of the person receiving it. Mothers like the one in Proverbs 31 can't always say things in a way that makes the person feel good or all warm and fuzzy. But just because it wasn't spoken in hushed, sweet tones doesn't mean it wasn't said in love.

What tone you take is almost as important as what you say. Keep that in mind as you weigh out the words you use in each situation.

Here are some more tips that will help you control your tongue and become more like the Proverbs 31 woman:

- Wait 5-10 seconds before saying what you want to say.
- Put yourself in the shoes of the people to whom you're talking. Ask yourself if what you will say will build them (or the person you're going to talk about to them) up or not. If not, don't say it.
- Consider if what you'll say might cause people to disrespect you. (Telling off-color or racist jokes, being crude, or saying things in a group to someone that should have been shared in private may cause people to lose respect for you.)
- Ask yourself if what you are about to repeat is gossip. If it is, don't say it.
- Examine the mental and physical state of the person to whom you are about to speak. If he or she appears distracted, angry, or upset, settling conflict or addressing issues shouldn't be the first thing out of your mouth. Show that you care by really listening.

And let's face it, some girls love drama. They like the pain their words inflict and the power it gives them. They like telling lies because they keep them out of trouble—for the time being at least.

Read Matthew 12:36-37, then answer these questions.

- ⁜ What do these verses have to say about careless words?

- ⁜ How does knowing you will be held accountable for your words challenge what you say and what you talk about?

- ⁜ How will knowing you'll be judged for your careless words change the way you speak to others?

GOING DEEPER:

- ⁜ It takes effort to guard your mouth. But 1 Peter 3:10-12 says that it's worth it. Write those verses below in your own words.

- ⁜ How will you strive to live out these verses this week? Write your action plan below.

- ⁜ This week we've learned that our words are powerful, and it's up to us whether we'll use them for good or for evil. Proverbs 18:21 says "Life and death are in the power of the tongue, and those who love it will eat its fruit." Life and death. Both come from your tongue. Which one will you choose? Why?

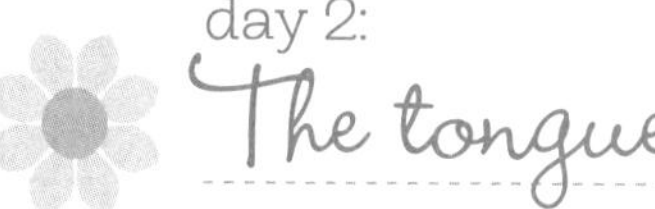

day 2: The tongue

Have you ever spent any time looking at your tongue? It's the strongest muscle in your body, although it's certainly not the biggest. It's a little weird looking. Sometimes it seems to have a mind of its own, doesn't it? You say something and wonder where those words even came from, don't you?

The good news is that this problem isn't new. The bad news is that you have to do something about it.

Read James 3:1-12. Answer these questions:

- What is the tongue compared to in verses 3-5? Why do you think the author chose those things?

- How does verse 6 change your opinion of the tongue?

- Verses 7-8 say that no one can tame the tongue. How have you found that to be true? What does that mean? Who **can** tame the tongue?

- According to verse 8, what is your tongue full of? How do you know that's true?

- Do verses 9 and 10 ever play out in your life? When was the last time this happened?

- What will you do today to prevent your tongue from continuing its "pollution" or "corruption" (v. 6)?

GOING DEEPER:

- After reading today's Scripture, draw a picture below of how you now see your tongue. (Make it as serious or as funny as you'd like.)

- James 3:8 says no man can tame the tongue. That's true. But you've got more than a man on your side to help you. How can God help you tame your tongue? What steps will you take to allow Him to do so?

- Spend some time confessing the sins you've committed with your mouth and ask God to tame your tongue. You may want to write your prayer in the space below.

day 3

Gossip

For many girls, one of the biggest sins involving our mouths is gossip. Do you know other girls who spend a lot of time talking negatively about others? Do you? It's easy to get caught up in the latest gossip, be it about the girl who's in your homeroom class or the starlet in Hollywood.

But is gossiping the best use of your words? Definitely not.

Please read Proverbs 11:13; 26:20-22. Answer these questions:

- According to Proverbs 11:13, what's the difference between a gossip and a trustworthy person?

- Which one would you say you are? Explain.

- Have you ever had a secret revealed about you? If so, how did that feel?

- Have you ever revealed a secret someone else told you not to share? What happened? How did it affect your relationship with that person? What did you learn about gossip from that experience?

- What is the relationship between gossip and conflict at your school? (See Prov. 26:20.)

- How can Proverbs 26:20 be useful to you as you deal with gossip at school?

GOING DEEPER:

- Choose a couple of verses from today's Scripture passages to write in your own words below. Consider making them into a sign to hang in your locker as a reminder of how to stop gossip at school.

- How can you stop gossip in its tracks? List some ideas for actions you will take this week when the opportunity to gossip arises.

- Will you commit to guarding your mouth from speaking gossip and to also protect your ears from hearing it? Why or why not? If you choose to do so, write your commitment below. Include specific ways you will avoid or refuse to speak or listen to gossip. Share your commitment with a godly friend who can hold you accountable!

day 4

Crude speech

Crude speech is unbecoming to a woman. Cursing, saying inappropriate things (especially when both guys and girls are present), and coarse joking do not reflect well on you or the God you say you serve. Sure, people may laugh or give you the reaction you were looking for, but speaking in such a way may cast doubt on your God-given intelligence and your commitment to Christ. We've been given more than a quarter of a million words in the English language. There are plenty of words to help you get your point across without making others cringe.

Read Ephesians 4:29; 5:4; James 5:12. Answer these questions:

- What is unwholesome talk or foul language? What's the big deal with talking like that?

- What do the students in your school consider to be unwholesome talk or foul language?

⁂ According to Ephesians 4:29, what should the things you say do? Explain what that might look like in your life.

⁂ Why do you think Ephesians 5:4 says coarse and foolish talking or crude joking are not suitable for believers?

⁂ When do you feel tempted to use coarse language, foolish talking, and/or dirty jokes? How can you choose to honor God when those temptations arise?

⁂ What should come out of your mouth instead of these things? Why?

⁂ How is it possible to let your "yes" be "yes" and your "no" be "no" as discussed in James 5:12?

(Being a person of your word will enable others to take you at your word. Basically, always tell the truth and follow through with what you say you'll do.)

GOING DEEPER:

- Do you struggle with cursing or saying inappropriate or crude things? Why do you think that is? When is the struggle the hardest? Why?

- If so, are you willing to ask God to put a filter in your mind so that you can catch those words before they come out of your mouth? Why or why not? If so, why not ask Him now? Write your prayer below.

- In addition to asking for God's help, what other practical steps will you take to make sure your talk matches up with your walk?

- How can you let other believers know when their speech crosses the line? Jot down a few ideas below.

day 5

Lying

Do you struggle with lying? Even little white lies, half truths, not telling the whole story, or not sharing all the details (especially with your parents) are still lies. Lying is proof of Satan's influence in our lives. (See John 8:44.)

So, what's the remedy so that we may speak truth at all times?

Read Proverbs 12:19; Ephesians 4:22-25, then answer these questions:

- Ultimately, how long does truth last, according to Proverbs 12:19?
- How long do lies last?
- Have you taken off the old you, spoken of in Ephesians 4:22? Why or why not?
- How can you be renewed in the spirit of your mind (v. 23)? Have you experienced that renewal? Explain.
- Have you put on the new (wo)man yet? In what ways do you share God's likeness?
- You're called to embody the "purity of the truth." Is it hard for you to speak the truth? Why or why not?

GOING DEEPER

- Write down your reflections on this statement:
  "A lie makes a problem part of the future. Telling the truth makes it part of the past."

- In what areas of your life is it easiest to slip into lies and untruths? Identify them below.

- How can you put Ephesians 4:25 into action today in those areas? Take steps not only to put away lying, but also to speak the truth! Write your ideas below.

day 6

When to speak, when to be silent

Our words can be so helpful. They can also be very hurtful. It's up to you to guard your tongue and make sure that the words coming out of your mouth are full of wisdom, like the Proverbs 31 woman. The Bible has a lot to say on this topic, so let's dig in.

Read Ecclesiastes 3:7b; Proverbs 12:18; 13:3; 17:27-28; 18:2,4,6-7,13; and James 1:26. Answer these questions:

- Why do you think Ecclesiastes 3:7b says there is a time to speak and a time to be silent? Which would you say you do more often? Why?

- Proverbs 12:18; 13:3; and 18:6-7 all deal with guarding your words in order to protect yourself. When have you experienced trouble because you didn't think before you spoke and said something you shouldn't have?

- In Proverbs 17:27 and 18:13, you learned that conversations are not just about saying the first thing that pops in your head. What do these verses teach you about how to act when you're speaking with someone?

- Compare the "fool" in Proverbs 17:28 and 18:2. Which one are you like more often?

- Are you like the person in Proverbs 18:4, whose words are a "fountain of wisdom"? If not, what can you do to become someone whose words are full of wisdom? (For a definition of wisdom, see page 12.)

GOING DEEPER

- Proverbs 18:13 contains a great lesson that many girls need to learn. Where or when do you have a hard time listening?

- What steps will you take to become a better listener? Write them below.

- James 1:26 is a hard verse to swallow. What is your response to it? Do you have a problem with controlling your tongue? Write about a recent time when you didn't control your tongue. What happened? What did you learn? What steps will you take this week to begin controlling your tongue?

day 7

A day for reflection

Read the following Scriptures and write about each of them, explaining to God how these verses had an impact on you:

- Proverbs 16:28

- Proverbs 18:7

> Her sons rise up and call her blessed. Her husband also praises her: "Many women are capable, but you surpass them all!" Charm is deceptive and beauty is fleeting, but a woman who fears the Lord will be praised. Give her the reward of her labor, and let her works praise her at the city gates.
>
> —Proverbs 31:28-31

week 9 appreciated

INTRODUCTION TO WEEK 9

Mother's Day isn't the only day you should let your mom know how much you appreciate her. Your mom (and dad, too) does more for you than you probably realize. Think about all the things your mom does for you. Does she cook some of your meals? Does she drive you to practices or pick you up from your friend's house? Does she work to help provide for your needs? Is your mom your biggest fan and encourager?

The fact is, moms are important people. Whether you always get along or you're currently convinced your mom is from another planet, she's still your mom. According to Scripture, our parents are supposed to be the people who shape us spiritually and teach us about life (Deut. 6).

Scripture isn't silent on how children should treat their parents, either. Remember the Ten Commandments, especially that one about honoring your mother and father (Ex. 20:12)? Check out Colossians 3:20. What does it say?

> "Children, obey your parents in everything, for this pleases the Lord."
> —Colossians 3:20

Clearly, God created the parent-child relationship, and it pleases Him when we respect, honor, and obey our parents. Parents aren't perfect people. They make mistakes—sometimes big ones. And while you may think your parents seem more flawed than other people's, you're still called to respect them, honor them, and obey them as a child of God.

But let's be honest: part of growing up is learning by example—and some moms simply haven't exactly set the best example. That's why we're studying the Proverbs 31 woman: she sets a great example of a godly woman for us. But you can also look at the women around you for examples of how life can be lived. The thing is, you must honestly evaluate what you see.

Consider your mom and possibly the moms of your close friends. If none of those options seem right, think about a godly, Christian woman you know.

- What do you like about these women?
- What do these moms do well?
- Without mentioning names, what don't they do well?
- In what ways would you like to be like them one day?
- What are some things that you might do differently than your mom (or other moms) in your life and with your own kids in the future?

Learning from others enables us to be better. Glean the good from their lives and imitate it in your own life. Learn from the mistakes they've made and don't repeat them. Who knows, one day *your* family may be rising up, praising you, and calling you blessed!

THIS WEEK'S THEME

Over the past few weeks, you've read Proverbs 31:10-31 numerous times. Do it one last time. After you've read the entire passage, focus on Proverbs 31:28-31.

> "Her sons rise up and call her blessed. Her husband also praises her: 'Many women are capable, but you surpass them all!' Charm is deceptive and beauty is fleeting, but a woman who fears the LORD will be praised. Give her the reward of her labor, and let her works praise her at the city gates." —Proverbs 31:28-31.

Basically, these verses are saying that a woman who works hard should feel appreciated and praised, especially by those who benefit from her labor. The lesson here is that beauty doesn't last, charm can deceive, but a godly woman of character isn't easily forgotten or overlooked. She's a hard worker, trustworthy, devoted to helping others, speaks wisely, and isn't overcome by fear or worry. She knows who God is and has allowed Him His rightful place in her life.

Because of these qualities and characteristics, these verses help us to understand that a godly woman's family should take the time to thank and praise her. Remember, this proverb was written to young men; it served as a reminder to them to love and cherish and praise their wives. But also, the verse is a reminder to young women to let their works speak for themselves. We are not to seek praise for ourselves and our actions. (So, no bragging on yourself!) We should let the praise find us, and it will when others see our good works and express their approval.

But here's the catch and the true identifier of our character: When you receive praise, do you take it all for yourself? Or do you point to God as the One who gave you the ability to do the things that garnered praise for you, thus glorifying Him? Like a mirror, our lives should reflect Christ in all that we do, and we should reflect any praise we get back to Him.

How can you be a mirror for God? Embracing the qualities of the Proverbs 31 woman is a great place to start!

day 1

A praiseworthy woman

You've seen the protagonist in Proverbs 31 work hard as you've studied her. You've watched her spin wool, purchase and plant a vineyard, prepare food, oversee lessons for her children, work late into the night, reach out to the poor, sell goods, clothe her family, and lovingly and wisely instruct others. Today you'll study how her family acknowledged her efforts and how this proverb ends. *(We realize that not every girl has a mom in her life, for whatever reason. It's our prayer that you do have a godly, influential woman who fills that role in your life. When we refer to moms in this session, we're also including this important woman.)*

Please read Proverbs 31:28-29. Answer these questions:

- Who praises the woman?

- Does she seek out the praise herself? Do you? Explain.

- When was the last time you took the lead in praising your mom?

- Does your family make the effort to let each member know he or she is appreciated? Why or why not?

- Do you see any of the qualities of the Proverbs 31 woman in your own mom?

- What do you love about your mom?

- How has she helped you become who you are today?

- Do you think your mom deserves some praise similar to what the Proverbs 31 woman received? Why? How would you praise her?

DO IT TODAY!

Write your mom (or whatever woman is most important to you) a letter, praising her and telling her why you're grateful to have her in your life. Reference the Proverbs 31 woman and cite examples of how she is like that woman. Leave the card somewhere she can find it.

You only have two more verses to cover in this entire passage. Can you believe you've been studying it for nine weeks? What have you learned? Record your thoughts below.

Read Proverbs 31:30-31. These two verses form the summary and conclusion of the passage. They are not a continuation of the family's praise. What these concluding verses are saying is that looks alone are not a reason for a man to choose a wife. While charm and beauty are not bad things, a woman's fear of the Lord should be the primary factor when a godly man chooses a wife.

Great looks are gifts from God, but they fade. Don't bank on them. Instead, seek to become a godly woman. Developing a healthy fear of God should be your primary concern. As a by-product, godly men will notice your virtues. The benefit of having a fear of the Lord will lead to more than marriage; Proverbs 30:30 says it will lead others to praise you. While we shouldn't seek praise, walking humbly with God will cause others to notice our lives and respect us.

- Verse 31 says that the woman should be given the reward of her labor and that her works will praise her at the city gates. What do you think this verse means?

GOING DEEPER:

- Take the time this week to thank your mom or a godly woman in your life, to encourage her, and to help her. Encourage your friends to do the same for their moms and help your family spend more time than usual appreciating your mom. (Don't neglect your dad as you do it, though!) If possible, plan a special outing for just you and your mom (or another godly woman) this week. Maybe you could go on a hike at a nearby park or have a picnic one afternoon. Pedicures, shopping, movies . . . the possibilities are endless, but just make sure she feels loved and appreciated! Write some ideas below.

WEEKLY MEMORY VERSE:

"So we must not get tired of doing good, for we will reap at the proper time if we don't give up." —Galatians 6:9

* What are some godly qualities you appreciate about your mom or mentor? How will you tell her so this week?

* Evaluate your life. Would your friends and family praise you for possessing any of the characteristics the Proverbs 31 woman displays? Why or why not?

* What qualities do you need to develop more in your life, even if it doesn't earn the appreciation or notoriety of beauty or charm?

day 2: Family relationships

Perhaps your family doesn't look like the one in Proverbs 31:28-29. Maybe it does. But every relationship can be improved. Think about your family. What issues cause problems in your family? What do you argue about? As you study the following Scripture passages, envision how you'll put them into practice in your family.

Read Ephesians 6:2-3 and Philippians 1:3-5. Answer these questions:

* Why does God command us to honor our parents? What does it really mean to honor your parents?

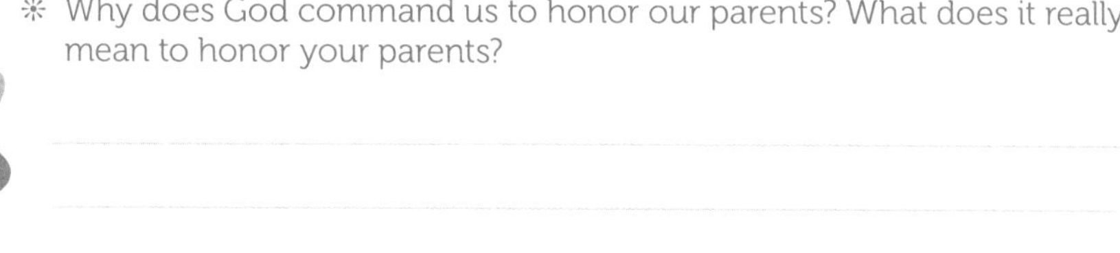

- How hard is it for you to honor your mother and father? Why?

- How can you honor your mother and father today? Be specific!

- What is the reward for doing so, according to Ephesians 6:3?

- Does anyone in your family come to mind when you read Philippians 1:3-5? Who? Why?

- Do you pray for your family like Paul said he prayed for other believers in Philippians 1:3-5? Why or why not?

GOING DEEPER:

- Has prayer ever changed a situation in your family? If so, what was that like? If not, why do you think that is?

- What are some specific barriers that keep your family from getting along? Write a prayer asking God to be present in those situations. Tell Him about the problems, how you feel, and why you need His help in those situations.

- No matter how "religious" (or non-religious) your family is, praying for them is always a good thing. Write down ways you can pray for your family and keep track of those requests. Ask your parents and siblings how you can pray for them. You may even want to start a family prayer time if your family doesn't already pray aloud together on a regular basis.

day 3

Do your parents set a godly example for you? If they do, you should consider yourself very blessed. If they do not, then you should know that we all have a perfect example to follow: God. His love is perfect, never-ending, and sacrificial. Even the best parents' love can't measure up to His. So no matter whose example you're following, you should be most focused on imitating His.

Please read Ephesians 5:1-5, then answer these questions:

- Have you ever seen a child imitate someone older than him or her? Why did Paul used that same imagery in verse 1?

- What do you think it will look like for you to imitate God?

- How can you "walk in love" today, like verse 2 tells you? List several practical ideas.

- What behaviors should you avoid (and definitely not imitate), according to verses 3-5?

- Are any of those behaviors present in your life? Which ones? What steps will you take to leave them behind?

- Rewrite verse 3 in your own words.

GOING DEEPER:

- In Ephesians 5:3, it says that sexual immorality, impurity, and greed should not even be heard of in you. Is there a hint of those things in your life? Explain. Be honest! What steps will you take to rid your life of these things?

- ※ Reread verse 5 aloud. Does that verse make you reconsider any parts of your life? Which ones? What changes will you make to ensure that your inheritance in heaven is not at stake?

- ※ Do you have someone in your life who is actively helping you follow Christ and become a godly young woman? Why or why not? Consider the godly women you know. Whom can you ask to be your mentor if you don't already have one? Why?

day 4

Hard work isn't easy

We know from studying the Proverbs 31 woman that she wasn't lazy. She worked long hours, put thought and effort into her days, and loved well. None of that comes easily. Her determination is obvious because it paid off. We know this because she was praised for her good works. But we all know that sometimes we get tired. We want to give up on the project, chore, or person because the task is taking a lot longer than we expected.

Read Galatians 6:9-10 and Ephesians 4:1. Answer these questions:

- ※ When have you gotten tired of doing the right thing? Why? What happened as a result?

- Why does Galatians 6:9 say we shouldn't give up on doing good?

- Why do you think Paul described himself as a "prisoner for the Lord" in Ephesians 4:1? What does that even mean?

- What does it mean to "walk worthy of the calling you have received"?

- In what parts of your life are you walking worthy?

- In what parts of your life are you not walking worthy? Explain.

GOING DEEPER:

- Name some areas in which you have potential (skills, talents, traits, etc.):

- ⁕ What steps will you take to develop those skills, talents, and traits to reach your potential in those areas?

- ⁕ Do you ever get tired of waiting to reach your potential? Why or why not? How will you prepare now for those times when you get tired of doing good?

- ⁕ What things in your life do you need to be more persistent about? Why? How will you do so?

day 5:

Recap: Part 1

We're almost completely through with this study. I want you to spend today revisiting the first half of the Scripture passage we studied in Proverbs 31 and learn from the woman portrayed in that passage.

Read Proverbs 31:10-22, then answer the following questions:

- ⁕ Why is a capable wife a precious thing to her husband?

- ⁕ Why do you think her husband trusted her?

- What do you think this woman's typical day was like?

- Describe or draw what you think this woman was like.

- What does this woman's desire to reach out to the poor reveal about her?

- Why did the woman not worry?

GOING DEEPER

- How are you like the Proverbs 31 woman?

- How are you different from her?

- In what parts of your life do you think God would like for you to become more like her? What steps are you taking to do so?

- How would this woman's life be different if she were alive today?

day 6

Recap: Part 2

Tomorrow is your final day studying the capable woman of Proverbs 31 and how we can incorporate her attributes into our lives. Thank you so much for hanging in there and digging in the Word as you become a girl after God's own heart. He has so much in store for you! Today we'll look once more at the woman in Proverbs 31.

Read Proverbs 31:23-31, then answer these questions.

- Based on what you learned in week 7, what kind of guy are you interested in marrying one day? How will that affect whom you'll date now?

* Are your words spoken with wisdom and in love? Why or why not?

* What's the difference between being idle and resting? Explain. (See verse 27.)

* Why is it important not to place your value in your looks?

* Are you living your life in a way that will cause others to praise you? Are you living your life in a way that will cause others to praise God? Why or why not?

* When you receive praise, what do you do with it?

GOING DEEPER

* One final question: How can your life glorify God? Think of all the different ways your life can bring honor to Him today and write about them below.

* Write a letter to yourself from God about what you just told Him. What would He say to you about the ways you want to glorify Him today?

day 7

A day for reflection

Read the following Scriptures and write about each below, explaining to God how these verses made an impact on you. Record what they taught you, how they changed you, and any new insights you had as you read them:

- Matthew 5:14-16

- Acts 9:36-42

- 1 Timothy 5:25

- Hebrews 10:24-25

for girls who want to lead a **Her** Bible study:

teaching plans

If you're willing to take this Bible study to the next level, consider going through *Her* again with a group of girls. Whether they're your age or younger than you, be prepared for God to speak to you in new ways as you study the Proverbs 31 woman with other girls.

If you're willing to lead such a group, plan to meet weekly. If possible, locate a room at your church with comfortable couches where you can meet. Or find a family who is willing to open their home to your group once a week. Consistency is important, so make sure you're cleared to meet there for the entire nine weeks of the study.

Prior to each week's group meeting, read through the teaching plans to make sure you have all the supplies you'll need and are ready to lead. You'll usually need paper, something for you and the other girls to write with, and a few other supplies, so make sure you set aside some time to prepare and gather the things you need.

When you meet for the study, you and your friends will go through each session's introduction as a group, studying the Scripture together and reading aloud the portions that resonated with you. You should also spend some time reading Proverbs 31:10-22, concentrating on the focal verse for each week. Challenge each other to commit these verses to memory, along with the weekly memory verses you'll find at the end of Day 1's work for each week of the study. You and the girls in your group will complete Days 1 through 7 of that week on your own before the next group meeting. (If you follow the teaching plan, you will actually end up doing a few activities from Day 1 during the group time each week.)

On the next few pages, we've provided a few activities, discussion questions, and prayer ideas for each week's meeting time. During the rest of the week, each member of the group will work through the remaining days of the week on her own in the *Her* journal. Be sure to allot some time during each weekly meeting to allow girls to share what they learned during their personal Bible study during the week.

week 1 The basics

MAKE THE INTRODUCTIONS

Before the first meeting, make sure each girl in your Bible study knows to bring a copy of *Her* (or you can purchase them for the girls ahead of time and distribute them at the meeting).

When the girls arrive, introduce them to one another. Be sure to have nametags available and plan to serve some snacks. Ask each girl for her contact information.

Once everyone has found a seat, **SAY: Each week we will study a different section of Proverbs 31. On the first day of each week's study we'll introduce the week's topic and dig into the sections of Proverbs 31 that teach us about it. Then, during the rest of the days that week, you'll discover more about the lesson to be learned in that section of Scripture by looking at the topic elsewhere in the Bible. There's a memory verse to learn each week, a lot of questions for you to think about, and some deeper questions for you to journal about in this book.**

Take time to read this week's introduction on pages 6-7 together and discuss this week's theme.

THE ONE

SAY: Proverbs 31 was written as a poem of instruction for young men. The writer was telling young men about the qualities they should look for when seeking a wife.

ASK: Do you think it's important to know some qualities that all guys worth marrying are looking for in the woman they want to marry? If you were to write a job description for the ideal wife based on the guys you know right now, what would it include?

Provide paper and instruct girls to create a job description for the perfect wife. Allow girls time to work, then ask a few to share their responses. As a group, discuss which qualities you believe are most important for a good woman or wife to have.

After discussing the qualities of a good woman, direct girls to work as a group to write a job description for the ideal husband. As they work, encourage girls to discuss why they believe these qualities are important in a husband.

A GOOD WOMAN

As the leader of the group, stress that the woman described in Proverbs 31 isn't real; she's an embodiment of every good quality in a woman. On a large sheet of paper, write *Proverbs 31 Woman.* **SAY: At the beginning of each meeting, we'll list a characteristic of the Proverbs 31 woman we discovered in that week's study. We'll compare the Proverbs 31 list to our concept of a good woman and see the similarities and differences.**

COMPARE/CONTRAST

Before the session, gather several copies of fashion magazines. As you leaf through the magazines, encourage your friends to look at the photographs of the celebrities, models, and actors. Discuss your favorite outfits, hairstyles, and so forth.

ASK: Do you compare yourself to other girls a lot? What does that do to your self-esteem?

Allow time for a short discussion about the dangers of always comparing ourselves to others and the damage it can do to our self-esteem. Stress that this study isn't about comparing ourselves to the Proverbs 31 woman in order to destroy our self-esteem or make us feel like failures. The focus of this study is to examine Proverbs 31 in order to learn the characteristics and qualities of a godly woman and develop them in our own lives.

SAY: Don't worry about trying to copy the Proverbs 31 woman. We should strive to be like her, but not worry over doing everything she managed to do.

A WISE WOMAN

Instruct a girl to look up James 1:5 and read it aloud. **SAY: In James 1:5, we are told that if we lack wisdom, we should ask God, who gives to all generously and without criticizing, and it will be given to us!**

Ask for a show of hands of who would like a little help in making decisions. Stress that God truly gives wisdom to those who ask for it. Invite the girls to join you in prayer as you ask God for wisdom for everyone in the room.

THE PROVERBS 31 WOMAN

Direct girls to take turns reading Proverbs 31 aloud, starting at verse 10. Have each girl read one verse. After the entire passage has been read, **ASK:**

- **What stood out to you about the woman?**
- **What surprised you about her?**
- **What did you like about her?**
- **What didn't you like?**
- **Why do you think her husband married her?**
- **How would a woman be more precious than jewels to her husband?**

CLOSING

Introduce a discussion question to wrap up this week's group study. **ASK: What do you hope to get out of this Bible study?** Write the answers on poster board and keep this list until the end of the study.

Close with a special prayer time in which you ask God's blessing on your Bible study group during the next nine weeks. Consider having girls join hands during this prayer. Remind girls to take time to complete each day's worth of study over the next week.

week 2: Being trustworthy

THE OPENING

When you're ready to begin Bible study, challenge the girls to say James 1:5-8, the memory verse from the previous week, together. Then give them a few minutes to share any insights they gained from their personal Bible study last week.

ASK: What characteristics of the Proverbs 31 woman did you discover in your study this week? Write the girls' findings on the large piece of paper labeled *Proverbs 31 Woman.* Discuss these characteristics and the standard for women God has laid out in Scripture.

Take time to read over this week's introduction on pages 22-23 and discuss this week's theme.

TRUSTWORTHY

ASK: What are some characteristics or qualities of a trustworthy person? As a group, list the qualities on a sheet of paper. Discuss the kinds of people who invite your trust. Direct a girl to read Proverbs 31:11-12 aloud. Afterward, **ASK:**

- **What exactly is trust, and why is it so important?**
- **How important is it that you trust your best friend?**
- **Do you think girls are more trustworthy than guys? Why or why not?**
- **Why is it key for guys to see that a girl is trustworthy?**
- **In what ways do we prove that we are not trustworthy?**
- **Why might showing that you're not trustworthy keep a guy from wanting to be around you?**

NOT TRUSTWORTHY

Distribute a piece of paper to each girl and make markers available. Instruct the girls to think about a time when someone broke their trust and draw something that symbolizes the way they felt during that experience. Allow girls time to work, and if they feel comfortable, ask a few girls to share their artwork with the group. When they have finished, **SAY: Not everyone is trustworthy. Most people will let you down. If you've been let down, you're not the first one who's felt frustrated with the lack of trustworthy people around her. A psalmist wrote about this thousands of years ago.**

Enlist a girl to read Psalm 9:1-10. When she has finished, repeat verse 10 aloud for the group. **SAY: The psalmist was remembering an experience in which he was dealing with an enemy and things seemed pretty hopeless. But God worked then, and He's still working today. He is trustworthy, and He is not going to break your trust. He is good because He is love. Tell God that you trust His provision and His timing. He'll prove His trustworthiness in time. And you'll have plenty of opportunities to prove yours.**

GOD'S CHARACTER

Instruct the girls to turn their artwork over and begin listing the characteristics that make them special. Explain that a characteristic is something that is always true and is an identifying feature of a person. Allow girls a few minutes to work, then ask each girl to share a few of the characteristics she listed. Discuss by asking:

- **What do your characteristics say about you?**
- **Why are your characteristics important?**
- **What are some of God's characteristics?**

Explain that God always acts out of His character. He is holy; therefore He can't be a part of sin and requires us to live holy lives. He is loving, so He sent us a Savior. **SAY: One of God's characteristics is that He is trustworthy.** Remind the girls of the drawings they created in the last activity. **ASK: How did God prove Himself faithful to you in that situation? How has He proven Himself trustworthy to you?** Allow time for a few girls to give personal testimonies.

PUT IT INTO PRACTICE

SAY: So how can we be trustworthy? Being trustworthy requires a determination to maintain a confidence and not gossip. It involves controlling your tongue so that you don't lie or deceive others. It means you do what you say you will, follow through on your commitments, and keep your promises.

Group girls into teams of two or three and give each team one of the following scenarios. Challenge them to come up with (and possibly act out) ways to be trustworthy in that scenario.

- **You have a friend who constantly gossips.**
  (Possible solution: Don't sit with her, or if you must, try to change the subject.)
- **You are tempted to lie to your teacher when she asked if you did your own homework because you know you just copied someone else's.**
  (Possible solution: Next time, how about doing your homework when you get home and not immediately getting online or turning on the TV? If not, shouldn't you tell the truth?)
- **Your parents are frustrated with you because your car needs an oil change, and you keep saying you "forgot" to take it in, but really you just didn't take it in because there was something more fun going on after school.**
  (Possible solution: Taking the car in like you said you would and seeing if you can meet up with your friends later.)

CLOSING

End the meeting with a discussion question. **ASK: What are some other practical things you can do to be trustworthy?** Allow girls to answer, then instruct them to look up and read aloud Proverbs 11:13; Psalm 34:13; Proverbs 12:19 for scriptural advice.

As you close in prayer, encourage the girls to write down any prayer requests they may have on an index card or scrap of paper. Direct them to exchange cards with other group members (or you can take them all up and distribute them at random) and instruct girls to pray for the requests on the card they received. Close in prayer (or allow a volunteer to), asking God's help for each girl to be more trustworthy.

week 3 Diligence

THE OPENING

When you're ready to begin Bible study, challenge the girls to say Proverbs 11:13, the memory verse from the previous week, aloud together. Encourage one another to keep committing these verses to memory, stressing how Scripture memorization is an important part of growing in relationship with God. Then, ask girls to share any insights they gained from their personal Bible study last week.

ASK: What characteristics of the Proverbs 31 woman did you discover in your study this week? Write the girls' findings on the large piece of paper labeled *Proverbs 31 Woman* you created in your first session. Discuss these characteristics and how you've seen them displayed in other women's lives this week.

Take time to read over this week's introduction on pages 38-39 and discuss this week's theme.

A HARD WORKIN' WOMAN

On a sheet of paper, draw a stick figure. As a group, work together to list the characteristics and qualities of a hard worker. Write the characteristics around the stick figure, placing them near the part of the body a hard worker might use to fulfill that characteristic. *(For example: A hard worker uses her time wisely should be placed near the stick figure's wrist. Girls could even draw a watch. A hard worker has a good attitude might be placed near the stick figures head, and so forth.)* After you and the girls have listed several characteristics, continue the discussion by **ASKING:**

- **Who's the hardest worker you know?**
- **What about this person keeps him or her focused on his or her task?**
- **Why do you think he or she works so hard?**

Enlist another girl to read aloud Proverbs 31:13-15,27. Discuss the verses as a group. Use the following questions to personalize your discussion:

- **What does the last part of verse 13 say?**
- **When was the last time you were eager to work?**
- **Do you ever take pleasure in your work? Explain.**

HOW DOES IT FEEL?

Group girls into two or three teams and assign each team a task. The task could be as simple as building a castle with building blocks or creating a necklace from paper clips. Prior to your meeting, secretly enlist one girl in each group to complain and procrastinate the entire time her team is doing the task. Allow the girls time to work, about three to five minutes. Debrief by asking:

- **How did her lack of work make you feel?**
- **When have you acted like she did, but in real life?**

Allow for a short time of discussion in which girls can share about times when their work ethic hasn't been very good. Do not allow the discussion to become a time to share horror stories about working in groups. Instead, direct girls' attention to verses 15 and 27 by reading them aloud. **ASK:**

- **How early do you think this woman got up?**
- **What was she doing that early in the morning?**
- **Whom was she feeding?**
- **What can you infer about her since she made sure her servants were fed?**
- **Why do you think verse 27 says she is never idle?**
- **How does her attitude differ from the attitude of the lazy girls in the activity we just completed?**

VARIETY IS THE SPICE OF LIFE

Direct a girl to read aloud Proverbs 31:14 again. **SAY: Here we learn that our protagonist is a hard worker who gets up early and brings variety to her life and the lives of those who live with her. I get the feeling that she's capable, confident, and loving.**

As a group, discuss ways you could introduce more variety into your lives and those of your families and friends. But don't just talk about it! Make arrangements to get together in the next two weeks to try some new things and embrace variety like the Proverbs 31 woman did. Here are some suggestions:

- arrange to go to dinner at a new restaurant sometime in the coming week.
- teach them to cook a dish they've never made before at your house.
- bring in new foods that they may have never tried before to your next session.

CLOSING

End your time together with a discussion of the Proverbs 31 woman and what you're learning from her. **ASK:**

- **What do you think about her?**
- **What do you like best about her so far?**
- **How are you striving to be like her?**

Explain that your closing prayer will be a popcorn prayer this week. You will open the prayer time by thanking God for the variety He gives us to enjoy in life.

Then, allow time for girls to pray aloud as they feel led. Allow as many girls as feel comfortable to pray, then close the prayer time by asking God to continue to teach you about the kind of women He is calling you to be and guide you as you continue your study of Proverbs 31.

week 4
Smart and strong

THE OPENING

As you begin this week's session, call for the girls to say last week's memory verse, Philippians 2:14-15, together from memory. Encourage girls to discuss what this verse has come to mean to them personally over the last week. Allow that discussion to lead into talking about any insights your group members may have gained from their personal Bible study last week.

ASK: What characteristics of the Proverbs 31 woman did you discover in your study this week? Write the girls' findings on the large piece of paper labeled *Proverbs 31 Woman* as you've done each week, then discuss these characteristics and how they apply to your daily life.

Take time to read over this week's introduction on pages 55-56 and discuss this week's theme.

BUYER'S REMORSE

Prior to the session, gather catalogs or open your laptop to a favorite online shopping site. Direct girls to page through the magazines or look through the site together and talk about items they'd like to buy. After a few minutes of discussion, **ASK:**

- **What about you? What was the last thing you bought?**
- **How long did you consider the purchase before you made it?**
- **Is that how you typically buy things?**
- **Are you usually satisfied with your purchases, or do you end up returning or not using the majority of things you buy?**

After talking over the group's answers, enlist a few group members to take turns reading Proverbs 31:16-19,22,24. **SAY: In verse 16, it says, "She considers a field and buys it; she plants a vineyard with her earnings." Basically, the woman in Proverbs 31 thought about her decision.**

As a group, talk about times you've bought something and later regretted it. Discuss how the principle of thinking through our purchases or actions could apply in other areas of life.

WHAT TO WEAR?

Call for a girl to read aloud Proverbs 31:19. **SAY: We're back to spinning! The author was intentional in bringing this up once more because it refers back to what a hard worker she is, starting with verse 13. She is engaged in the making of clothing for her family, and sets about the task often.**

Challenge the girls in your group to imagine that they couldn't go to the store to buy clothes. **ASK: What would you do? How would you make clothing for yourself?**

Distribute paper and art supplies and instruct girls to draw what kind of clothes they'd make if they couldn't go shopping. Provide old magazines and catalogs for girls who'd rather make a collage of ideas than draw. Allow time for everyone to work, then call for girls to present their creations.

After the presentations, remind girls that during the time period in which Proverbs was written, clothing was made using distaff and spindle, a time-intensive process that predates even the spinning wheel! Research distaff and spindle prior to your meeting so that you can help the girls have a better idea of the work that went into making clothes back then. If the laptop is handy, you may even want to show them a few pictures of distaff and spindle from a trusted site. **SAY: Understanding that it took a lot of time to make clothes back then, what this verse is really saying is that the Proverbs 31 woman was an extremely hard worker.**

STRONG ARMS

Instruct the girls to flex their biceps. **ASK: How strong are your arms?** Allow for a few minutes of discussion (and laughter), then invite a girl to read aloud Proverbs 31:17. **SAY: Proverbs 31 says our capable woman had strong arms, likely from all that hard work she was doing.** As a group, discuss the importance of taking care of your bodies. Create a list of practical things you can do this week to make healthier choices and take care of the body God has given you. Urge each girl to write the list on the back of their drawings from the previous activity and circle two ideas they will commit to do this week. Challenge girls to sign the page as a symbol of their commitment and share that commitment with another girl in the group who can hold them accountable this week.

THE CLOSING

End the meeting by saying: **Like the Proverbs 31 woman, God has blessed you with a brain that He'd like you to use. If He's given you arms and legs that work, He wants you to use them. God has uniquely gifted you to do things others can't.** Challenge the girls in your group by **ASKING: Where can you work and serve and give Him glory (instead of keeping it for yourself)?**

Allow time for a short discussion, then begin your closing prayer time by asking the girls to share prayer requests. Close in prayer, instructing each girl to pray (either aloud or silently) for the girl on her left.

Remind girls to do each day's worth of study over the next week and be prepared to share what they learned during the week.

Leader Note: *Next week's lesson is about serving the poor. Work out details this week for a service opportunity for you and the girls, to be announced during next week's meeting.*

week 5 Love for others

THE OPENING

Begin the session by urging the girls in your group to join you in saying Galatians 6:9 aloud together. Then, challenge your brains by trying to repeat the four previous memory verses. Encourage one another to continue committing God's Word to memory.

Begin this week's discussion by enlisting girls to share any insights they gained from their personal Bible study during the last week. Allow time for discussion, then **ASK: What characteristics of the Proverbs 31 woman did you discover in your study this week?** Write the girls' findings on the large piece of paper labeled *Proverbs 31 Woman* you created in the first session, comparing it to the list of characteristics of an ideal wife you developed in the same session. Once again, discuss any characteristics or qualities that appear on both lists.

Take time to read over this week's introduction on pages 71-72 and discuss this week's theme.

REACH OUT

Enlist a girl to read aloud Proverbs 31:19-20. **SAY: Last week, verse 19 left us watching this woman reaching out to grasp her spinning staff, hard at work in her home. Like a good movie director, the writer then switches the action, but her hands are still in the same position. We're transitioned to seeing her use her hands in another context: loving the poor.**

Call attention to the wording used in the Scripture: the Proverbs 31 woman "reached out" to the poor. **ASK: How does that wording suggest the Proverbs 31 woman's actions were deliberate?**

Group girls into pairs and challenge them to list as many ideas for ways to serve, give, and otherwise deliberately reach out to the poor in their schools, community, and world as they can in three minutes. Provide paper and pens to each pair. When time is up, discuss the girls' ideas. Challenge the girls to prayerfully consider making at least one or two of the ideas a reality in their lives.

End this activity by telling the story of Katie, a girl in her 20s from Brentwood, Tennessee, who lives in Uganda and has adopted 14 girls and feeds hundreds more starving children every week. Check out her story at *kissesfromkatie.blogspot.com.*

EXCUSES, EXCUSES

Call attention to Proverbs 31:20 again, stressing that the woman was actively reaching out to help the poor and needy. **ASK: Why do we avoid helping the poor?**

As girls call out their answers, record them on a large sheet of paper titled *"Excuses: Why we avoid helping the poor."* After you have listed several excuses on the sheet of paper, discuss them, talking about their validity and how excuses sometimes stop us from doing what we know we should or what God has called us to do. As a group, commit to stop buying the excuses and start doing what's right.

Prior to the session, enlist at least four girls to act out Matthew 25:31-46. (Parts: Narrator, Jesus, the "righteous" on the right, the "unrighteous" on the left) After their presentation **ASK: To Jesus, how important is helping people in need? How important should it be to us?**

Inform the girls that you have set up an opportunity to serve people in need. Explain where you'll be going and hand out permission forms.

ACT IT OUT!

Group the girls into four teams and instruct them to read over their assigned passage of Scripture. Allot time for teams to read and prepare, then call for presentations. Stress that teams should act out what happened in the passage.

Team 1: Matthew 8:1-4 (2 people)
After the team acts out the passage, **ask the entire group:**
- **What was wrong with the man?**
- **What did Jesus do that would have been shocking to the Jews then?** *(Read Leviticus 13, especially verses 45-46 and also see Isaiah 52:11 to see why touching an "unclean" man was so taboo.)*
- **What happened to the man?**
- **How was Jesus' interaction a good example for us?** *(Touching those the*

world considers untouchable gives them hope, makes them feel valuable [Hey! I'm worth touching!], and extends grace to them.)

Team 2: Matthew 8:14-17 (4 or more)
After the team acts out the passage, **ASK the entire group:**
- **Where was Jesus when this healing took place?**
- **What might have He preferred to do at that moment?** *(sit down, relax, eat)*
- **What did Jesus do in order to heal her?** *(He touched her.)*
- **What did He do later that day?** *(Healed the demon-possessed and the sick.)*

Team 3: Read Matthew 9:27-33 (4 people)
After the group acts out the passage, **ask the entire group:**
- **What was wrong with these two guys?**
- **What did Jesus ask them?**
- **How did He heal them?**
- **What did He tell them not to do?**
- **What did they do?**
- **What was wrong with the other guy who appeared later in the story?**
- **What happened after Jesus drove out the demon?**

Team 4: Read Luke 13:10-13 (2 people)
After the team acts out the passage, **ASK the entire group:**
- **What was wrong with this woman?**
- **How did Jesus heal this woman?**
- **How long did it take for her to be restored?**

THE CLOSING

End the session by **ASKING: What response do you have to seeing how Jesus loved and served others?** Allow time for girls to talk about their thoughts, then distribute a blank piece of paper and a pen to each girl. Explain that you'll end this week's meeting by writing a prayer to Jesus about their toward people in need. Encourage girls to find a place in the room where they can have some privacy, then allow time for them to write their prayers. End the time by praying aloud, asking God to open your eyes to the needs of those around you.

week 6

Not anxious about the future

THE OPENING

As you begin this week's session, challenge the girls to say James 2:15-17, the memory verse from the previous week, aloud together. Talk together about what that verse has come to mean to you over the week. Then attempt to recall the previous memory verses. Encourage the girls not to give up on memorizing Scripture, even if it seems difficult.

Allow girls to discuss any insights they gained from their personal Bible study last week. **ASK: What characteristics of the Proverbs 31 woman did you discover in your study this week?** Write the girls' findings on the large piece of paper labeled *Proverbs 31 Woman* as you've done each week, then talk about practical ways you can embody those characteristics. Take time to read this week's introduction on pages 89-90 and discuss the theme.

WHAT ABOUT THE FUTURE?

ASK: How much time do you spend thinking about the future? Allow girls time to respond, then **ASK: When you think about your future, what do you think about? What are your biggest concerns?** As the girls call out their responses, write a one-word description of each concern on an index card. After several concerns have been mentioned, **SAY: As females, it's easy to live in a dream world of future possibilities. No matter how far into the future you let your mind wander, don't get too far ahead of yourself. Today, we'll see how the Proverbs 31 woman handled things beyond her control, including the future.**

ALWAYS BE PREPARED

Direct a girl to read aloud Proverbs 31:21,25. Call attention to verse 21. **SAY: We know that she spent a large part of her time making clothes. And her household was reaping the benefits: they are not cold because they were "doubly" clothed.**

ASK: Have you ever not been dressed right for the weather? Allow time for a few responses, then enlist a girl to look up the forecast for the next day on a laptop or her phone. Instruct her to read the forecast aloud as you distribute old catalogs or fashion magazines. Group girls into pairs and provide each pair with a piece of paper, a marker, scissors, and glue or tape. Challenge girls to create an outfit using photos from the magazines that they would wear for the kind of weather the forecast predicted. Allow 5 to 10 minutes for girls to work, then call for teams to present their creations.

After each team has shared, explain that the Proverbs 31 woman wasn't worried because she was prepared. Remind girls of the concerns they listed in the previous activity. Pick one or two of the worries (particularly ones that you know are going to happen, like an upcoming exam or tryout) and discuss practical ways you could be better prepared to face them when they actually do happen. **ASK: How does being better prepared for something take some of the worry and stress away?**

PUT IT ON

Call attention to Proverbs 31:25 by enlisting another girl to read it aloud. **SAY: Verse 25 reveals the true character of this woman. "Strength and honor are her clothing, and she can laugh at the time to come." In addition to the physical clothes she put on each morning, this woman also clothed herself in strength and honor.**

Direct girls' attention to the activity on page 91 about what we're to put on as believers. Assign each Scripture to a girl (or group of girls) and allow them to work. After a few minutes, call them together and call for girls to share their answers with the group. Talk together about practical ways you can "dress" yourself in these qualities and characteristics every day.

IN CONTROL

SAY: An interesting fact about the Proverbs 31 woman is found in verse 25: "She can laugh at the time to come." This woman has worked hard each day to prepare for whatever the future might bring. If something crazy happens, then she can probably handle it (and even laugh at it). But even if it's beyond her control, she knows who's got it under control.

ASK: Do you ever forget who's in control of your future? In what way? Why? Allow time for girls to share, then instruct girls to look up Matthew 6:25-34 in their Bibles. Enlist a girl (or girls) to read the passage aloud.

After the girls have read the passage, say: **If you forget who actually has the future under control, you may cross the line into obsessing about the future. If you're letting your worry over the future affect today, that's clearly not the way Jesus intends for you to live.**

While the girls have their Bibles open to Matthew 6:25-34, challenge them to write a few of the things they're worrying about in the margins around that Scripture. They can list things you've talked about earlier in the session or things no one else knows about. **SAY: I want you to write down the things that worry you—big deals, small issues, whatever. If it worries you, write it down, along with the date. Then, every few months, review this list. See how God has taken care of the things that worry you.**

THE CLOSING

Wrap up this week's discussion by **ASKING: Why do you think some people worry so much? If you struggle with worry, how can we as a group help and hold you accountable to Jesus' teachings?** Allow time for girls to discuss why they worry and offer suggestions to help one another, then call attention back to the stack of index cards you created in an earlier activity. Challenge girls to pick the worry that stresses them out the most. Explain that you'll end this week's session by praying over these worries and diligently seeking God's power in the middle of them. Allow girls time to pray individually, then close by asking God to give you all courage to release your worries to Him. When you've concluded your prayer time, place a box or wastebasket in the center of the group. Tell them they can symbolically hand their worries over to Christ by placing the index cards in that box or basket.

Leader's Note*: At the end of the first day's study, girls will be asked to write down the things that worry them. It's a good idea to assign prayer partners from within the group who can pray with them and for them in the coming week about those specific worries.*

THE OPENING

Begin by inviting the girls to say last week's memory verse, Philippians 4:6, aloud together. Enlist a few girls to share what God taught them through that verse this week and spend a few minutes discussing it.

ASK: What characteristics of the Proverbs 31 woman did you discover in your study this week? Write the girls' findings on the large piece of paper labeled *Proverbs 31 Woman*. Discuss these concepts and how this study is challenging your concept of what it means to be a godly woman. Read this week's introduction on pages 106-107 and discuss this week's theme.

THE QUALIFICATIONS

Invite a girl to read aloud Proverbs 31:23, then remind the group that Proverbs 31 was written as advice to young men. **SAY: We're at the middle of this passage, the hinge. Verse 23 is directed at the poem's audience, young men. The verse we just read is a charge to each man that he aspire to be esteemed even by his elders and earn a position of respect in the city.**

Talk together about the kind of men the girls in your group suggest, focusing on men who embody the characteristics of this verse: gaining the respect of other men and earning a place of honor in their church, community, or state. **SAY: Chances are that the guys we're around are still immature at times, are not in positions of power in our town, and are just trying to get through school with passing grades—not find a wife of noble character!**

Remind the girls of the job description of an ideal husband that you created in your first meeting. Discuss how today's verse changes or affects the description you wrote six weeks ago. Direct the girls' attention to the list of important qualities on page 106, then ask them to think about guys they know who possess these qualities now. **ASK: Which of these qualities do you think are most important for a guy to have? Why? Do you know any grown men who possess some of these qualities? How do those qualities define their lives? Do you know any guys our age who are working to develop these qualities?**

WHO HE'S NOT

Enlist another girl to read Proverbs 31:23 again. Stress that it's important to note that this verse is not telling us to seek to marry someone who is well-known or wealthy. The fact is, the well-known and the wealthy in our society often don't have these qualities.

Show girls a magazine devoted to celebrities, like *People* or *Us Weekly*, or visit their websites. Challenge the girls to think about the celebrity crushes they've had, then **ASK:**

- **What types of relationships are those guys in now?**
- **Why are those guys well known?**
- **Are they intelligent?**
- **Are they full of integrity?**
- **Are they disciplined?**
- **Are they diligent?**
- **Are they wise?**
- **Are they determined?**
- **Most importantly, are they godly?**
- **What kind of qualities should you be looking for in a man?**

Explain that the reason we're attracted to a guy shouldn't just be his popularity or if he's well-known or wealthy. **SAY: Even now, we should be interested in dating guys who love God and seek to let Him shine in their lives.**

THIS ONE'S FOR THE BOYS

ASK: So if you were the author of Proverbs and were writing it to young women, what would you say? Group girls into teams of two or three and instruct them to look over Proverbs 31:10-31 and write an outline to help young women find the type of man who qualifies as a "Capable Husband" in God's eyes. Provide paper for each team. Allow girls several minutes to work, then call for the teams to share what they've written.

AN EVALUATION

Instruct girls to turn to page 108-109 for a quiz. Challenge each girl to work individually and answer the questions about the guy she currently likes most.

Give the girls time to work, then **SAY: If you answered no to that last question, I want you to take steps this week to remedy the situation or end the relationship/infatuation with the guy. Why waste your time with the wrong guy?**

This isn't the time for an extended discussion of guys or to list what's wrong with the guys your friends are interested in or are dating. Simply ask this question and encourage the girls in your group to really think about and pray over this question during the next week. Stress that you will be available after the session and during the week to anyone who wants to talk.

THE CLOSING

End the session by asking a girl to read aloud Ephesians 5:22-31, then wrap up this week's session by **ASKING: Why is dating guys who are respectable (and respectful of you!) important?** Allow time for discussion, then close in prayer by allowing girls to pray in groups of two or three, sharing their requests and interceding for each other as they seek to become godly women.

week 8 Wise Words

THE OPENING

Start the session by challenging the girls to recite 1 Timothy 6:11, last week's memory verse, together. Make it even more of a challenge by attempting to recite all the previous week's memory verses without looking.

Invite the girls to share any insights they gained from their personal Bible study during the last week, then **ASK: What characteristics of the Proverbs 31 woman did you discover in your study this week?** Write the girls' findings on the large piece of paper labeled *Proverbs 31 Woman* you created in your first session, then discuss the new additions. Take time to read over this week's introduction on pages 123-124 and discuss this week's theme.

WORDS MEAN SOMETHING

Begin the session by encouraging girls to talk about the power of our words. Invite participation and allow time for girls to discuss the following questions. **ASK:**

- **Have you ever been wounded by words?**
- **Ever been the victim of gossip?**
- **Have you ever wounded others with your words? If so, how?**
- **On the other side, do you have any words of encouragement from someone important that you like to recall and repeat to yourself when you're feeling down or discouraged?**
- **When have you seen your positive words completely turn a situation around?**

Stress that our words are so powerful and can be used for good or for evil. **SAY: Let's look at how the Proverbs 31 woman used her words.** Enlist a girl to read aloud Proverbs 31:26. Point out that the woman in Proverbs 31 thought carefully about not only what she would say, but also when and how she would say it. **ASK: How carefully do you think about what you say? What about when and how you say things?**

WATCH YOUR MOUTH!

Invite a girl to read aloud James 3:5-8, then **SAY: We all know that it's not easy to control the tongue.** Read aloud James 1:26, then **ASK: Why is it important that we control our tongues?**

Allow time for responses, then **SAY: Every time you speak without thinking and utter unwise words in an attempt to tear down others, build yourself up, or win an argument, you discredit yourself and the God you claim to serve.**

WHAT ARE YOU LETTING IN?

SAY: Maybe it's the way you say things that gets you in trouble. Proverbs 21:23 says, "The one who guards his mouth and tongue keeps himself out of trouble." How do we guard our mouths? The answer may surprise you, but you guard your mouth by guarding your heart. Remind the girls of Matthew 12:34 and Luke 6:45, which you read in the introduction to this week's theme.

SAY: The things you store in your heart and surround yourself with will influence what words come out of your mouth. Prior to the session, research the current top downloaded song, the movie with the best ticket sales, and the best-selling teen book. Group girls into three teams and provide them with the titles of these releases and a short synopsis or description. Encourage teams to discuss the media they've been assigned, identifying topics or themes presented in them that fly in the face of God's truth or His standard. Allow time for discussion, then call for each team to present its movie, book, or song, detailing the themes they identified. As each group concludes, **ASK: How could these things influence your speech or behavior? ASK: How have you seen movies, music, friends' language, books, and so forth influence your speech—for good or for bad?** Allow time for discussion.

Challenge the girls to honestly evaluate the voices they've allowed into their lives that lead them away from God's truth and influence their speech and behavior. Encourage girls to honestly confess them to God. Distribute a few sticky notes to each girl and instruct her to write Proverbs 21:23 on each sticky note, then to place them as reminders on items in her life that symbolize the areas she identified in her personal prayer time *(i.e. putting the verse on her TV to remind her to guard her heart with what she watches; placing the verse on her laptop or iPod to remind her to guard her heart with the music she listens to, and so forth).*

THE CLOSING

Close in prayer this week by setting up four prayer stations around the room.

• At one station, display pictures of things that might inspire girls to adore God. *(Photographs of nature's beauty, friends, family, delicious food, etc. could help.)* Place a large poster board and pens or markers nearby and leave a notecard instructing girls to record their praise of God for who He is and what He's done and can do on the poster board.

• At another station, include a stack of papers and pens and encourage girls to confess their sins. Instruct them, through a notecard left at the station, to list their sins (including their careless words!) on the paper(s), ask for God's forgiveness for each sin, and then dispose of the paper(s) to represent their repentance. Leave a trashcan nearby. You can allow girls to choose to discard their sins by shredding them with scissors, crumpling them up, or by tearing them into tiny pieces.

• At another station, create a list on which girls can write what they're thankful for. Expressing our thanks to God is a good reminder to us of who's in charge. Encourage girls to take as long as they need to write down how God has blessed, provided for, or taught them.

• At one station, leave a candle burning, along with a note instructing girls to lift up their prayer requests and the needs of others. This station is about supplication—especially for others. God knows our needs and loves to hear the hearts of His children.

Allow girls as much time as they need to move through the stations. If possible, play some quiet music as they move through the stations.

***Note to leader**: Next week's lesson references a mother-daughter event to take place at some point after next week's meeting. Begin planning that event. (Ideas include a pottery-painting time, cooking class, tea, makeover, and so forth.)*

week 9 Appreciated

THE OPENING

Begin the session by urging the girls in your group to join you in saying James 1:26, the memory verse from the previous week, together. Begin the discussion by enlisting girls to share any insights they gained from their personal Bible study during the last week. Allow time for discussion, then **ASK: What characteristics of the Proverbs 31 woman did you discover in your study this week?** Write the girls' findings on the large piece of paper labeled *Proverbs 31 Woman* you created in the first session, discussing these new additions to the list and how they affect the way you live your life. Take time to read over this week's introduction on pages 140-141 and discuss this week's theme.

ALL ABOUT MOM

Prior to the session, instruct girls to bring a photo of their mom (or a godly woman in their lives) to this week's meeting. Invite each girl to show her photo to the group and explain why she chose that picture of her mom. After the girls have shared, direct them to place the photos in front of them, where they will be able to look at them throughout the session. Provide each girl with a sheet of paper and a pen, then **ASK: Do you see any of the qualities of the Proverbs 31 woman in your own mom? What do you love about your mom?** Instruct girls to write the qualities of the Proverbs 31 woman that they see in their own moms or the things they love about their mom on the sheet of paper you've provided. Allow girls time to work, then discuss their findings. After each girl has shared, enlist a volunteer to read aloud Proverbs 31:28-31, then **ASK:**

- **When was the last time you took the lead in praising your mom?**
- **Does your family make the effort to let each member know he or she is appreciated? Explain.**
- **How has your mom or dad helped you become who you are today?**

Stress once again that Proverbs 31 was written with young men in mind, and these verses clearly describe the kind of woman a young man wants to have in his life. The lesson here is that beauty doesn't last and charm deceives, but a godly woman isn't easily forgotten or overlooked. Nor should she be. **SAY: A woman who embodies the characteristics of the Proverbs 31 woman should be appreciated for her character and hard work. ASK: Do you think your mom deserves some praise similar to what the Proverbs 31 woman received?**

PUT IT INTO WORDS

Direct girls' attention to the photo of their moms they brought with them to the session. Distribute note cards (or let girls make their own out of paper and art supplies) and instruct each girl to write a letter to her mother or a godly woman who is important in her life, praising that person and telling her why she's grateful to have her in her life. Challenge the girls to reference the Proverbs 31 woman and cite examples of how the women they're writing to are like that woman. Tell girls to take the cards home and leave them somewhere their moms can find them. You may also offer to mail the cards for the girls.

TALK IT OUT

Guide the girls in your group in a discussion by instructing them to consider their moms and other godly women in their lives as they answer the following questions:

- **What do you like about these women?**
- **What do these moms do well?**
- **In what ways would you like to be like them one day?**
- **What are some things that you might do differently than your mom (or other moms) in your life and with your own kids in the future?**

SAY: In celebration of your mom and all she's done for you, we're going to have a mother-daughter event. In the past week, you should have planned a special time together for moms and daughters, such as a pottery-painting party, a cooking class, a special dinner, or something else your group will enjoy. Give the girls the details at this time. Be sensitive to any girls in the group who may not have a mom and encourage them to invite a woman (grandmother, aunt, foster mom, teacher) who is important to them to come to this event.

MIRROR, MIRROR

Call for a volunteer to read aloud Proverbs 31:30-31, then **SAY: Verse 31 says that the woman should be given the reward of her labor and that her works will praise her at the city gates. What do you think this verse means?**

Allow for a time of discussion, in which you remind the girls that this proverb was written to young men and these verses served to remind them to love, cherish, and praise their wives. **SAY: But also, the verse is a reminder to young women to let their works speak for themselves. We are not to seek praise for ourselves and our actions. We should let the praise find us, and it will when others see our good works and express their approval.**

ASK: When you receive praise, do you take it all for yourself? Or do you point to God as the One who gave you the ability to do those things?

THE CLOSING

SAY: Like a mirror, our lives should reflect Christ in all that we do, and we should reflect any praise we get back to Him. Prior to the session, obtain a full-length mirror and dry-erase markers. **ASK: How can you be a reflection of God?** Invite each girl to look at her reflection and write her answer in dry erase marker on the mirror.

Close the session with a special prayer and affirmation time. Place a chair in the center of the room. Instruct a girl to sit in it while the rest of the group gathers around her and lays their hands on her. Begin the prayer time yourself by praising God for that girl and her special attributes, then open it up to her peers. Repeat this process for each girl in your group. *(If you have girls who are a little afraid of praying in public, enlist a few volunteers before you begin each girl's prayer time so there isn't awkward silence and the girl being prayed for doesn't feel as if no one wants to pray for her.)* Giving girls the opportunity to pray for and encourage their friends will create unity among the girls in this study. Don't be surprised if they're ready to do another Bible study as soon as you finish this one!

with your mom

Girls, if you want a deeper connection with your mom (or another important, older godly woman in your life), then use *Her* to get there! We've provided some discussion questions and activities to do together over the coming 9 weeks as you both study this material. These activities should be done at the beginning of the each week's study. We recommend that you do them either just before or just after you complete "Day 1" of each week. Further your study by committing to memorize each week's memory verse together. Make sure your mom has her own copy of *Her*. *(We realize that not every girl has a mom in her life, but we do hope you have a godly, influential woman who fills that role. When we refer to "your mom" in this guide, we're also referring to that influential woman in your life.)*

WEEK 1: THE BASICS

Take turns reading aloud Proverbs 31:10-31 one verse at a time. Ask your mom:

- What do you think are some of the most important character traits for a godly woman?
- What should I be looking for in the guys I date?
- How do you think you're like the Proverbs 31 woman?
- How are you different from her?
- What traits in me do you see that look like her?

Tell your mom about the girls you compare yourself to and why. Help her understand what that does to your self-esteem. Ask her whom she compares herself to and why. Ask her how that affects the way she feels about herself.

Journal about what you learn. For the duration of this Bible study (and as long as you want to continue), create a prayer journal with your mom. Buy a pretty notebook or decorate one together, and record each other's prayer requests and the date you began praying about them. As you pray and God answers your prayers, record how He has worked. This journal will serve as a testament to the fact that God hears and answers your prayers.

WEEK 2: BEING TRUSTWORTHY

Read Proverbs 31:11-12 aloud. Then ask your mom:

- What exactly is trust, and why is it so important?
- How important is it that you trust your best friend?
- Why is it important for guys to see that a girl is trustworthy?
- In what ways do we prove that we are not trustworthy?
- When have I been trustworthy?
- When have I broken your trust?

Read Psalm 9:1-10 and focus on verse 10. Ask your mom to talk about a time when she doubted God's trustworthiness and what happened in that situation. Share with your mom what situation has made you doubt God's trustworthiness.

Pray for each other. In addition to writing down your prayer requests in the prayer journal this week, you and your mom should each write down your prayer requests on an index card. Switch cards and pray for each other's requests and for God's help to be more trustworthy. Then take your mom's card and put it somewhere you'll see it every day. Pray for her needs whenever you see that card, and ask her to do the same for you.

WEEK 3: DILIGENCE

Ask your mom:

- Who's the hardest worker you know?
- What about this person keeps him or her focused on the task at hand?
- Why do you think he or she works so hard?

(Feel free to answer the above questions yourself after your mom has shared her thoughts.)

Ask your mom to read aloud Proverbs 31:13-15,27. Discuss the following questions with your mom:

- How early do you think the woman in this passage got up?
- What was she doing that early in the morning?
- Whom was she feeding?
- What can you infer about her since she made sure her servants were fed?
- Why do you think verse 27 says she was never idle?

Pray together, thanking God for your hard-working mom. Ask your mom to pray over you as well. This week, commit to getting up early with your mom to pray over the day, study the Word, or just make breakfast together.

WEEK 4: SMART AND STRONG

Read Proverbs 31:16-19,22,24 aloud to you mom, then discuss verse 16, stressing that the Proverbs 31 woman clearly thought through her decisions. Ask your mom:

- What was the last thing you bought?
- How long did you consider the purchase before you made it?
- Is that how you typically buy things?
- Are you usually satisfied with your purchases, or do you end up returning or not using the majority of things you buy?
- Would you want me to shop or make purchases like you do? Why or why not?

Re-read verse 16, then discuss the following questions with your mom:

- Do we take care of ourselves, physically?
- Do we eat right?
- Do we exercise a few times a week?
- Do we get enough good sleep?
- How might taking care of ourselves be pleasing to God?
- What will we do this week to take better care of ourselves?

Pray for each other. Talk with your mom about the ways she sees you being able to work and serve and give God glory. Discuss the ways you see her doing the same thing. Close your time by praying for each other. Ask God to help you both use the gifts and talents He's given each of you to glorify Him.

WEEK 5: LOVE FOR OTHERS

Read Proverbs 31:19-20. Discuss the following questions with your mom:

- If she were alive today, how would the Proverbs 31 woman likely have reached out to the poor?
- Where might she have served?

- What might she have done for the needy?
- How many of those things are we doing?

Read John 13:1-15 together and discuss that passage. Talk about why Jesus washed the disciples' feet and why it was such an act of service. Discuss what it means to serve with an attitude like Christ's. Tell your mom about a time you've observed her serving others with a Christlike attitude. Ask her about a time she's seen you do the same.

With your mom, make plans to serve the poor, needy, or lonely together during the coming week. You two could knit baby blankets for a crisis pregnancy clinic or maternity home, offer to babysit for a single mom, arrange flowers and take them to residents at a nursing home (taking time to visit with the residents to whom you give the flowers), serve at a soup kitchen, and so forth. The opportunities are endless and could even become a weekly or monthly thing for you and your mom to do together!

WEEK 6: NOT ANXIOUS ABOUT THE FUTURE

Read Proverbs 31:21,25 aloud. Discuss the fact that the Proverbs 31 woman doesn't seem worried about the future. Tell your mom what you think about when you dream about your future (occupation, spouse, kids, car, travels). Ask your mom to share how she dreamed her life would be when she was your age. Compare and contrast her dreams with reality. Ask about her dreams now for the future.

Read Matthew 6:25-34 together. Discuss the following questions with your mom:

- What areas of life did Jesus address in this passage?
- Which of those things have you worried about before? Why?
- How do verses 33-34 speak to you in your worry?

Ask your mom: If you struggle with worry, how can I help you and hold you accountable to Jesus' teachings? After your mom has answered, share your answer. Write your worries in your prayer journal and take time right now to pray together and release your worries to God. *(If you'd like, write what is making you anxious or worried on a piece of paper or an index card. Pray, asking God to give you both courage to release your worries to Him. When you've concluded your prayer time, symbolically give your worries over to Christ by crumpling up and dropping your papers into a wastebasket or by burning them.)*

WEEK 7: THE RIGHT KIND OF GUY

Go get coffee (or any other snack you both enjoy) with your mom during your Bible study time. Find a cozy corner with comfy chairs or a booth. As you'll be talking about guys this week, you and your mom might want to observe any couples in the coffee shop or restaurant. Together, analyze what their relationship might be like by the way they interact.

Read Proverbs 31:23. Discuss with your mom that Proverbs 31 is directed at young men and this verse is a charge to the man that he aspire to be esteemed even by his elders and earn a position of respect in the city. Ask your mom to talk about which guys at your school or youth group she has noticed being respected by older men and why.

Look at the list of important qualities on page 106, then discuss with your mom why these qualities are important for a guy to have. Ask your mom to open up to you about any relationships with guys in her past in which the guy(s) didn't possess these qualities. Ask your mom how those guys acted and how they treated her.

Ask your mom to pray a special prayer over you in which she petitions God to guard your heart, to bring you a godly man in His timing, and to seek God and your parents' wisdom if you date.

WEEK 8: WISE WORDS

Talk with your mom about gossip. Ask your mom:

- Have you ever been wounded by words?
- Have you ever been the victim of gossip?
- Have you ever been called a name that left you crying in the bathroom?
- Have you ever wounded others with your words? If so, how?
- On the other hand, do you have any words of encouragement from someone important that you like to recall when you're feeling down or discouraged?
- When have you seen your positive words completely turn a situation around?

Encourage one another with art. Gather two pieces of scrapbook paper or cardstock, along with pens, markers, and art supplies. Direct your mom to write your name in the middle of her piece of paper, then write all the things she loves and admires about you around it. You should write your mom's name (or what you call her) in the middle of your sheet of paper, along with all the things you love and admire about her. Exchange these pages, then keep them somewhere safe. That way, when one of you has a bad day, you have a place to look for affirmation and encouragement.

Read James 3:5-8 and James 1:26 and discuss why it's important that we control our tongues. Discuss these questions with your mom:

- How can I do a better job of guarding my tongue?
- How have I hurt you with my words?
- When does the way I say things bother you?

WEEK 9: APPRECIATED

Show your appreciation to your mom. Read Proverbs 31:28-31 together, then use the following discussion points to actively express your appreciation to your mom:

- I see the following characteristics of the Proverbs 31 woman in you. . .
- What I love most about you is . . .
- Mom, here's how you've helped me become the person I am . . .
- Mom, you do these things really well . . .
- Someday, I'd like to be more like you in these ways . . .

Re-read verse 31 and discuss with your mom what you both think that passage means. Stress that the latter part of that verse is a reminder to young women to let their works speak for themselves. We are not to seek praise for ourselves and our actions. Discuss these questions with your mom:

- When you receive praise, do you take it all for yourself? Or do you point to God as the One who gave you the ability to do those things?
- Like a mirror, our lives should reflect Christ into all that we do, and we should reflect any praise we get back to Him. How can you be a mirror for God?

Take time this week to do something special with your mom. You can plan a surprise activity, or you can enlist her help to plan something you both will enjoy doing. If time and money allow, make plans to go on a mission trip with your mom. Some other fun things to consider doing together might include: painting pottery, getting a pedicure, watching a movie, volunteering, or whatever you two like to do!